Letters to my Broker
P.S. What do you think of the Market?

A. Kustomer and Clem Chambers

Illustrations by David Pinnell

ADVFN BOOKS

CONTENTS

INTRODUCTION

by Clem Chambers

There are only a tiny number of copies of this book that have survived the 93 years since it was printed. I bought it from a dealer for a significant amount of money to add to my collection of books on the market.

I was not expecting such a hilarious classic.

In 1928 Eddie Cantor, the great American comic of his time, is reputed to have said, "My broker told me to buy a stock and that I'd sleep like a baby. I did. I wake up every three hours crying." He may well have added other baby-like behaviour to the punch line but that hasn't come down to us.

This book is in the same humorous vein, but not only is it a piece of hilarious writing, it is packed with market insight.

The amazing thing about this ancient book about the stock market is that it is so fresh and so relevant. It could almost be a modern satire.

It seems so impossible that a 90-year-old book could be so relevant today and feel so contemporary that it feels like it should be a modern hoax. Can so very little have changed since 1919 that you can appreciate Joe's letters to his broker as if they were emails sent from a smartphone?

But **Letters to My Broker** is no hoax. This book, that catalogues the out of control behaviours of a trader, is a record not of today's market gamblers but of a speculator from just after World War I ended. It's a different world from today's high tech one, but not it seems for the trader.

For all the online trading technology, the overarching regulation, the thousands of educational books on investing, traders behave now exactly as they did 94 years ago. What is more, the results, losses and how they occur seem unchanged. It is like some steam-punk fantasy, without the fantasy.

I don't laugh at much; if something is funny I normally can raise a smile, but this book actually made me laugh out loud. It is perhaps the wicked way the author sends up himself (or perhaps his customers) with pinpoint accuracy, or perhaps, like all great satire, the way it strips away pomposity and humbug to reveal the sorry truth, which hits my funny bone. Yet it is not the humour wherein the value of this book lies. P.S. lays out the behaviours that cost so many novice investors and would-be traders so much of their hard earned capital. These losses were real then and are real now. They are as significant as they are unnecessary.

Goldman Sachs employees have been known to call their clients "muppets," which translated in trader speak means clueless participants. In the markets, clueless participants are lambs to the slaughter. Trading is a game of winners and losers and muppets don't stand a chance.

Letters illuminates this and gives insight into the mistakes of the novice.

It's hard to start in the market and not be such a lamb to the slaughter. This book gives you a master class in how muppets behave and what can happen to them. Novice and experienced investors can all benefit from this master class.

In the City of London, I recently saw a banner outside a poker room. It read, "Beginners welcome." That was also surely the case in

1919.

It doesn't need to be like this, but as this book shows, for the last 100 years at least, private investors have been falling into the same traps.

I decided to republish the book through ADVFN Books as ADVFN is a haven for private investors and traders. The world needs this book back in print before it is lost forever.

At the same time I decided to annotate the book and bring a perspective to the text while adding various insights to focus in on crucial issues.

Joe, the book's protagonist, is a wealthy man, but his Wall Street dealings aren't going the way he planned. Driven by the excitement of trading and the lure of easy money he is prepared to constantly come off on the wrong end of the deal, chasing the illusory market killing.

Joe isn't a tragic figure, not at all. He is a man who will never starve. He has skill, determination and smarts. He has built a small fortune in the rag trade. If he loses his shirt he can sow another. Yet somehow he can't get to beat the street and instead takes a thumping from the market time and again.

He is not a quitter, he is not sorry for himself, not for a New York minute.

This is New York in 1919. There is no safety net. There is no regulator. There are no insider trading rules. Wall Street is the Wild West, and meanwhile the Wild West is also still the Wild West. There is no one to go crying to if you lose; there is no social safety net. If you get ruined, you get ruined.

Yet for all the difference in times and safeguards, Joe behaves like any iPhone wielding day trader punting today on Pink Sheet stocks in New York, AIM in London or Mothers in Tokyo.

While generations have come and gone and the world has changed dramatically, the psychology, behaviour and fate of the "short life trader" has been left untouched.

This is a book to laugh with and to learn from.

It encapsulates all the emotions you will feel and many of the behaviours you will be tempted to follow. Through it you will meet the market scams that still haunt stock markets today even with the untold oversight set expensively to save us from such fraud.

It will tell you how not to invest and trade, which is as good as telling you what to do when it comes to overall profits.

Letters From my Broker is the classic investment book that nearly vanished from the record and I'm proud to bring it back for your enjoyment.

It is both a treasure and a treasury.

P.S. What do you think of the market?

JOE'S LETTERS

Atlantic City, April 14, 1919.

Dear Eddie:

Well, Eddie, I see the market went down again yesterday. That's all it seems to be doing lately. You've got me trading in two stocks, Eddie, which I'm calling after my two children – Fannie and Milton – God bless 'em . . . no matter what they do, it always costs me a lot of money.

Say, Eddie, who's been buying all this here Marines stock everybody's talking about, and if it is so good, why don't you buy some for me? You know Eddie, you can do anything you want in my account for me. Just use your own discretion, but let me know before you do anything.

A feller told me last night a deal was on in this Marine Company where the preferred gets $150 a share. If that's right and you can buy them for 110, there's $40 a share cinch ain't it, and on 50 shares that makes $2,000. Figure it out yourself, and if my figures are right, buy me 50 shares and send me a check for $2,000 by return mail.

How is my railroad stocks? You certainly steered me wrong when you said I should invest in St. Paul preferred because the Savings Banks wouldn't let it go down. What d'ye mean invest when no sooner you have bought it for me, your firm asks for more margin. If I had only followed Meyer Silver's advice and bought some of that Mexican Pete, I wouldn't be stopping at the dump I am, but a two room sweet at the Traymore would be more like it. What do they charge there?

Why is it your firm always charges me the highest interest, last month 7 per cent., when I can go to my bank downtown and borrow a line of my own statement which aint even audited and pay only 6 per cent. with a 1/2 per cent. extra for renewals. Maybe I should transfer my account, hey Eddie, or would you be angry? Anyway I shouldn't ask of you the question. Remember me to Sadie and tell her Flora was asking for her.

Yours, etc.

JOE.

P.S. Sell my Steel at the highest price to-morrow.

P.S. Don't forget about the Marines. Better send me only $1,000 and keep the other $1,000 in my account.

P.S. What do you think of the market?

Clem's Comment:

Nothing seems to change in stock market speculation, which is why ADVFN is publishing this ancient and obscure stock market book. It's a funny book, satire verging on the slapstick. If would be even funnier if people weren't acting the same way today as they did nearly a century ago. This is the lesson to be had by investors and traders alike. The mistakes that lose you money are basic. Avoid them and your chances to do very well improve dramatically.

As for Mexican Pete: Fresnillo, a Mexican silver mine, trades in London today but whether there is a modern Meyer out there to tip you is another matter.

Atlantic City, April 30, 1919.

Dear Eddie:

Well, Eddie, the market was dull today so the evening papers here say it, but all my stocks wasn't dull at all. They couldn't stay up if they was supported by sixteen airships. That's a fine bunch of junk you've bought for me. I ain't kicking y'understand Eddie, only it seems funny that all my friends here is making so much money they spend it like nothing, while I can't even make expenses. Maybe they deal with a first-class house, hey, Eddie?

Don't you think I should buy some Wilson & Co. stock? The prices they charge here for rooms and board is something fierce and Mrs. Epstein the prop. says that the price of meat is so high she can't do it for less, so I thought that people like Wilson & Co. should be making lots of money and if I buy some of the stock I'll get even for the high prices I pay to Mrs. Epstein, ain't it?

This morning I was interduced to a feller called Goldfogle, which is a friend of Hirsch whose brother is next to the Sumatra crowd. He told me absolutely confidentially Sumatra will sell at 200 before it goes down 5 points and then he buys himself 100 shares right in front of my face. Don't you think I should buy some too? Of course I wouldn't wait for 200 exactly. If I buy at 105 and sell at 175 that suits me. 70 points ain't so bad. Why should a person be a hog and wait for the last point? Put in a order for 100 or 75 shares, or if you don't like it so well make it 50 shares, but buy only 25 shares at a time. This feller Goldfogle is a big bluff. He says he'll blow the crowd to lunch and when we all walk up and down the boardwalk six times to get up an appetite y'understand, he beats it! Better not buy any Sumatra, I ain't got confidence in him anyways.

I didn't get my check for the Marines yet. Whats the matter with your firm Eddie, must the eagle scream before you let go of a dollar and oblige,

Yours truly,
JOE.

P.S. Goldfogle just phoned he was detained but will buy me a lunch to-morrow so you better buy 50 shares of that Sumatra stock.

P.S. Phone me to-morrow when the market is at the top.

P.S. Dave Wolf just came in from Cleveland. He sends his regards.

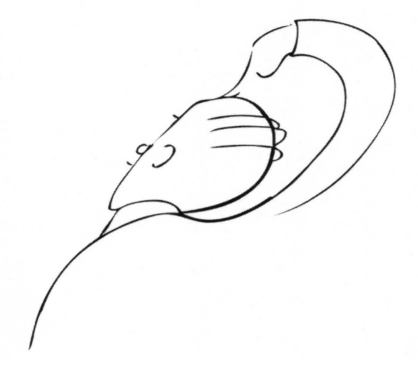

Clem's Comment:

Watch out for that Goldfogle. These days he would be called a ramper. There are plenty of rampers around. They will even take you to lunch unlike poor Joe.

The promise of knowing someone who knows the in-crowd is a typical lure. "A friend of a friend knows the guy and he says . . ." is about the best way on the planet to buy a market top and lose your shirt on the planet. What's more, if it was true it would be illegal insider trading.

If you shorted every inside tip you were given in a city pub, you would do very well indeed, because it is the lifeblood of speculation to "talk up your book" and there is always a poor Joe to take the bait.

Atlantic City, May 2, 1919.

Dear Eddie:

You better sell all my stocks for me as soon as you receive this letter. If you don't get it in the first mail, telephone me right away. Conditions don't look right to me, and I think this here League of Nations question a serious question. I heard a feller speak here last night in the Auditorium, and he certainly knows what he is talking about, which is more than some people I know, know. I aint referring to you at all, Eddie, but your judgment on the market aint been exactly right just the same.

Anyway, this speaker says the country is going to hell, and the laborer is going to run the nation if we don't look out, and maybe we will have a panic and strikes and everything. So you better sell all my stocks, but be careful and don't throw them overboard. The market may be strong tomorrow. It's always strong on Thursdays, ain't it, Eddie?

I'm awful nervous about conditions just the same. I got a letter from my partner today which says why don't I come back, because they want to strike in the pressing room, and with him trying to settle it why should I be loafing here with the rich. The nerve of him, Eddie, when last summer he takes his whole family to Averne and never even writes me a line for ten days. That's a partner for you.

I see by the papers where the Interborough went broke. The stock is selling so low at 3 that it looks like a real bargain. Don't you think I should buy some, because it's so low? They say that all the rich men bought when stocks was cheap and sold when they was dear. If that's right, why don't you buy some of this cheap stock for me, and buy any other cheap stock that's cheap, but don't pay more than $5 for it. That's enough to pay for a cheap stock. Your mother-in-law is here. She came last night. Did you know it, or is it a surprise?

Yours respectfully,
JOE.

P.S. What do you think of the market?
P.S. Send me a check for $100. Prices here are terrible.
P.S. Don't sell anything until I tell you.

Clem's Comment:

Joe is making the classic mistake of thinking a low priced share is cheap. I've even heard institution brokers say this today. "The share price is only a penny so it's easy for it to double."

Just for the record a $1 or 1p share is not cheap and a $500 or £30 share is not expensive. The main component of the cheap/expensive debate is market capitalisation, which is price x shares in issue. A cheap company is one you can buy for less than the company is worth, not the price of each share. Penny shares are often infinitely expensive as the companies like broke "Interborough" are worthless.

Atlantic City, May 14, 1919.

Dear Eddie:

I see the oil stocks are strong, All my friends is making thousands on oil stocks. Why didn't you tell me something about them instead of buying for me Marines and Sumatra and St. Paul preferred and all that dreck. If it wasn't that you was related on my wife's side I should have transferred my account long ago. I ain't criticizing you personally Eddie, y'understand, but I ain't exactly laughing all over since you make for me nothing but Irish dividends. Which reminds me that you called for margin again. Don't your firm get tired sending me notices when you know I'm good for it even if there ain't enough money in my account, which there must be since I aint drawn any money. Besides tell your credit man to look us up in Duns or maybe Bradstreets where our rating is $50,000 to $75,000 B2, which isn't so bad as we always pay thirty days.

I'm sick of Atlantic City. First I think I can go away and make my expenses fooling with the market, and find out that not only I lose money but it costs me the whole profit on a bill of goods I sold to Nathan & Kaplan, of Emporia, Pa., three weeks ago and which ain't even billed yet. Then my wife Flora meets her relations from St. Louis, and immediately she stays in the department stores so long I can't look her in the face when she comes back to the hotel. And my daughter spends $45 for one bathing suit which she never uses in the water, and cries because she cant ride on horses every morning. Such ideas they get when theyre away from 125 street!

I nearly forgot what I wanted to ask you. What do you think of the market? Should I sell or should I hold on? I heard a rumor that the market is going way up. Did you hear something? If you heard the same thing buy me some stocks that will go up only let me know before you do anything. I see United Cigar Stores sold at 135 yesterday. It cost me only 106 so I got a profit, aint it? I heard an old saying once that a feller never loses money taking a profit. Is that right? If it is then you can sell my stock for me at 137 but if it gets near there then dont sell but sell it a little higher. I'll be home soon if my family lets me, and let me know if there is anything new, and tell me about some stock that will go up like Mexican Pete. I want to show the boarders here something. Hoping you are the same,

Yours,
JOE.

P.S. Send me my mail in plain envelopes.
P.S. Better sell my Cigar Stores at the market, but not for less than 140.
P.S. Don't ask for no more margins.

Clem's Comment:

$45 on a bathing suit is about $3,000 in modern money (measured against the price of gold). A $3,000 bikini, does it exist today? You bet! Apparently it is called "The Anita." As with the market, so with fashion!

Joe is busy trying to chase the next big thing, but sadly it is the last big thing. Buy at the bottom and sell at the top is therefore inverted, he buys at the top and sells at the bottom. Meanwhile he has been lured into believing the big money is not in work and commerce but in speculation. He's a rich man, $50,000-75,000 is 2-3,000 ounces of gold – roughly $3-5m in today's money. For now at least he has the firepower to play and keep his brother in law in commission.

Atlantic City, May 20, 1919.

Dear Eddie:

I want some advice. Not that I'll follow it, because if I followed all your misinformation my creditors would be willing to settle for ten cents on the dollar without bankruptcy proceedings. Listen Eddie, what do they mean by going short on the market? They tried to explain it to me, but its like understanding the League of Nations. I don't get it.

Goldfogle, the feller I wrote you about who knows Hirsch whose brother is close to the Sumatra crowd, bothers the life out of me each day telling me now is the time to go short of the market. He says you sell something you aint got and buy it back when it is so much cheaper. How is that Eddie? When you aint got a thing how can you sell it, and if you never had it how can you buy it back? That feller is too slick for me. He says Barney Baruch made a fortune that way. Is that honest?

Simon Stein from the Steubenville Clothing Company, fine people, too, they always pay two off ten prompt, came here yesterday and right away he makes expenses buying some Union Pacific in the morning and selling it in the afternoon. He gets a check right away and didnt even put up a nickel, where I am putting up good money all the time and all I get is calls for more margin. Either some people have all the luck or I got a rotten broker, and I dont always believe in luck either.

Has my partner called you up Eddie? If he calls you don't tell him what I'm doing in the market for he always wants to copy me. I guess you can tell him about those stocks which has gone down on me but tell him nothing about those which went up. I guess you can tell him anything him wants to know. I guess you better make the account a joint one with my partner. He told me before I left anything I done was O.K. If he wants to know why we aint made no money tell him Eddie. You know why better than anyone else. Remember me to your father and tell him why don't his firm don't give us any business. We received a nice line of fall goods last week, and oblige,

Yours, etc.,

JOE.

P.S. Is it hard to go short?
P.S. I just sold Stein a bill of goods.
P.S. Don't forget to make it a joint account.

Clem's Comment:

Leverage kills. The more leverage you use the more likely volatility in the market will eat your margin and create the dreaded margin call. Margin costs too as the money you borrow for leverage is lent at interest. The deposit you put down is a deposit, so the 9 units you buy with your 1 unit of margin is charged at interest, say 7%. So the position has 7 x 9% interest on it – 63% annual interest. So if you hold the position for a year and the stock doesn't move, you just lost 63% of your capital on the deal.

"Do you want margin with that sir? Have a nice day!"

What is more there is nothing worse than a margin call. If you had the money spare it would be in your brokerage account.

Margin calls are what traders have nightmares about.

Atlantic City, May 22, 1919.

Dear Eddie:

How does my account stand now? I can never understand them trick statements your firm sends me every month. And then they want me to sign my name saying everything is O.K. I guess you must have something to do with those Statements, Eddie. Aint those your initials at the bottom, E. & O. E. Who is the other fellow?

Eddie, getting down to serious business, what do you think of the market? A feller what just came down for the week-end, and spends nothing but our time, says the tecknikle position of the market is weak. Is that serious Eddie, and will stocks go down much? You know I don't understand all those fancy things, and I didn't know there was anything tecknikle about the market, like architects and engineers and all those do-nothings. Let me know what it means when the tecknikle position is weak. When will it be strong again? Write me all about it.

What do you think about General Motors? Shapiro, which is the buyer for the Enterprise Department store in Detroit, says he heard a man saying on the train that the General Motors is buying up the Studebakers. Last night my wife's uncle, which is staying with us, at my expense, says the General Motors is buying Keystone Tire, and what do you think Eddie, this morning I met a feller on the board walk I ain't seen since the last lodge meeting, and he says they is buying up the Saxon, Peerless and Chandler. Can you beat it, Eddie? Next thing you know they'll be buying up Ford. Ain't it the limit?

Flora is feeling better today. We all took a salt water bath last night. You must do it sometime Eddie. They say its good for lumbago. Which reminds me that my partner has lumbago, so don't tell him about these here salt water baths. He might want to come down and then I must come back.

Yours,
JOE.

P.S. The evening paper says General Motors is negotiating for Ford. Aint I got the remarkable foresight?

P.S. Don't forget the tecknikle stuff.

P.S. If you think General Motors is going up, buy me 50 shares, but wait until it goes down first. They say it's bad to buy at the top.

Clem's Comment:

Errors and omissions excepted. It's still a sorry fact today that brokers' statements and portfolio reports can be confusing, misleading and wrong. A large, well known, broker who will remain nameless, to this day only gives a portfolio position at the close of the previous night which is barely any use at all. I use ADVFN's portfolio tracker that gives me real time results in multimarket multicurrency portfolios. You certainly need to know where you are, if like Joe you are leveraged long and the "tecknikles" are looking weak.

Atlantic City, May 29, 1919.

Dear Eddie:

Why don't you buy me some of these here peace stocks everybody is talking about? All the boarders here is buying peace stocks on their brokers advice, and I have yet to hear a word from you about them. Why don't you keep me posted? If you would only give my account some attention I could bring you some customers. I tried to get you a customer yesterday but he says he has to deal with another firm because his wife has relations in the business. I told him he has nothing on me, and if my wife has got relations in the pick-pocketing business I should have to help them also, which aint so far away from your line, hey Eddie?

I got your weekly market letter this morning. Say Eddie, who writes that stuff? With my compliments that feller could get a job writing the weather reports for all the good you get out of them. He don't say a thing but maybe it means something else. He always says that if the market don't go up maybe it should go down and if it rains next Tuesday the sidewalks will be wet. Does a feller what writes that stuff get paid for it, or is it done for amusement? Tell him for me he could make an honest living writing for Life or maybe the Ladies' Home Journal.

Is the market a buy? I got a peculiar feeling I should buy something. Did you ever have a peculiar feeling you must have some stocks before its too late? What's good in the market? Do you think the "Rails" is a good buy now? I want to feel how it feels to make some money. Just once! Buy me a good conservative stock like Pennsylvania. Buy 100 shares at the market. When I feel I want to buy a stock I never put a limit on it. Thats the only way to be. Take your time in buying this stock, Eddie, dont run after it. You always seem to buy for me at the top and sell for me at the bottom. If you do that again I will change my account, relations or no relations.

Yours,

JOE.

P.S. Don't buy that stock. The Pennsylvania had an accident this afternoon, which I see by the papers one man was hurt. Maybe the stock will go down now.

P.S. You haven't asked for more margin this week. Whats the matter? Is your firm flush?

P.S. Send me your market letter every week.

Clem's Comment:

Joe of course is a hopeless gambler. He is in an obvious co-dependant relationship with his broker and the market. He is a sucker for punishment. Most gamblers are. It's not the winning they crave but the release of pain and associated endorphins and the exhilaration of escape from dire losses.

In his PS he doesn't want to buy a railroad because of an accident. Perhaps he should buy it because the accident will artificially depress the price for a few days. But buying at the bottom and selling at the top is not for Joe.

Atlantic City, June 10, 1919.

Dear Eddie:

Why dont you ever put me in a Syndicate? All my friends have been making thousands out of Syndicates, and from you I dont hear a word. Dont your house ever have any syndicates? If you dont, let me know of some houses what has. They say its the easiest way to make money. You wait until they get up a syndicate, and then you say you want a piece of it, I think they call it a participation or some other fancy name, and then all you do is sign your name to some papers, and a few weeks later they send you a check which always has an uneven amount to show that they have deducted the expenses. Why don't your house do something like that? No wonder most people lose money in Wall Street. They don't know about this here syndicate business, which is where all the money goes. After this no stock market for me. I'm going to look out for one of those syndicates.

What do you think of the market? I read in this morning's papers that the Marine deal is off again or on again, I don't remember which. But that don't make any difference to that stock, does it Eddie? Believe me that stock acts like its got St. Valentines dance. Plenty of action I should say, but I wouldn't touch it with a fifteen foot pole. Its too risky. If a feller was on the right side of this here Marine, he could make a lot of money in one day, couldn't he, Eddie? Do you think I should try it just once? Suppose you buy me, say, 50 shares. Or maybe you should sell it. Let me know. Maybe you better phone me first, because my judgment far away maybe better than yours, who has his nose so close to the ticker its always black with ink, aint it?

Is Kirschbaum & Kahn a good reliable first class banking firm? How are they talked about in Wall Street? My daughter has been going around with young Sidney Kirschbaum since we came here, and while he or she aint said anything to me yet, y'understand, Flora thinks something may happen soon, so I want to be prepared. Dont say anything about it Eddie, not even to your own mother, because maybe nothing comes out of it. Hoping youre the same I am

Yours,

JOE.

P.S. Don't forget about Kirschbaum. He took Fannie to theatre last night and bought flowers and candy. He may say something soon.
P.S. Is he rich? He has a car with a funny name.
P.S. Look him up in Bradstreet. Also Dun and the A.B.A.

Clem's Comment:

Marine is volatile and to Joe whose nose isn't pressed to the ticker tape there seems no rhyme or reason to the swings in price. He is basically right, the price swings around randomly because the situation is uncertain and uncertainty is randomness is volatility.

There was no ADVFN real time streaming in 1919, instead when prices moved they were sent down the ticker and printed out of thin white strips of paper. This was such a common thing that the skies themselves could be filled with ticker tape, should a famous person ride down a New York street. Ticker tape and confetti seem to be in the air for Joe. His daughter may marry a banker; even in 1919 this wasn't necessarily a happy prospect.

Atlantic City, June 14, 1919.

Dear Eddie:

I have been getting a bunch of letters from a lot of Curb houses telling me to buy Omar Oil, Marsh Mining, and Perfection Tire, and a lot of other stocks. Are they any good, Eddie? Someone told me all these Curb houses is bucket shops and that a feller aint got no more chance of making money out of them than you have of becoming intelligent! What is a bucket shop anyways? Is it anything like a pool room where you play Daisy Gold to win and when she comes home with the money the house is raided by friends of the proprietor in policemen's uniforms, ain't it?

Such literature those curb houses send a feller. Every morning I get a letter from one house telling me whats good in the market. Funny, ain't it, they never say oser a word about what's bad. And when the stocks they say is good goes down do they say they was wrong? Not on your life. They say you must average, which means that you lose twice as much as you intended to. This average stuff is great for the brokers but rotten for the people. How is it Eddie, you aint never tried that average stuff on me, or was you going to try it soon? Don't do it, Eddie I warn you, for I close my account then and there at the first mention.

One house recommends Consolidated Ranger Oil Syndicate stock. That sounds like a good title. They say its only 25 cents a share and in two weeks it goes to 50 cents and the first of August it will be positively $1. How do they do it, Eddie? It looks like a sure thing. You know I dont believe in those kind of stocks, and wouldnt invest a nickel in a oil company unless it was something like Standard Oil of New Jersey which is so high I couldn't even pay the commission for buying it. Look into that oil stock I mentioned above, not that I'm interested in the least, but maybe there is something in it. My lumbago is fine. Hoping youre the same,

Yours,
JOE.

P.S. I bought some of that oil stock at 25 cents. Do you think I'm stuck?

P.S. The stock has a green border and a fine picture of a oil well.

P.S. Why shouldn't I sell them the stock back at $1 on July 1st? Maybe you better not wait and sell it at 50 cents or get me out even. I forgot to tell you I got only 100 shares.

Clem's Comment:

Stock spam . . . in 1919. These newsletters sound suspiciously like the equivalent of those emails we all get spammed with telling you to buy, buy, buy. The spammed stock of course collapses within hours. It is all part of a stock scam.

Boiler rooms, pink sheet rampers, selling useless stock is at least 94 years old and likely much older still. People still fall for it today.

The market has no memory.

The 'curb' is the curb on the pavement or sidewalk, as Joe would have called it. The OTC, the pink sheets, the grey sheets are today's equivalent of these curb stocks.

Joe is on the hunt for easy money and wants to get rich quick. Trying to get rich quick then and now is how people get poor fast. Joe is rich, but you wonder for how much longer.

If he had bought General Motors in 1919 and held it he would have likely had a better outcome. GM was a bubble stock in those days, worth $1 billion dollars, but even so, he was bound to have done better in GM than in a curb stock of dubious pedigree.

NB: From *Only Yesterday* by F L Allen 1931: "Never give up your position in a good stock." Everybody has heard how many millions a man would have made if he had bought a hundred shares of General Motors in 1919 and held on.

Atlantic City, June 30, 1919.

Dear Eddie:

I went to a fine dinner last night at the Breakers. Some swell affair, Eddie, with everybody wearing his wedding suit. Nearly everybody you know was there. Sam Rubin from Syracuse sat right next to me, and before he knowed it I had sold him a bill of goods which my partner couldn't have touched him with if he talked himself blue in the face.

Do you know Abe Feldenheimer from Savannah, Eddie? A nice fine feller, which has lots of money. He told me he buys something now and then so I told him when he goes to New York to see you and say I sent you. If he does some business don't you think you should lower my interest rate? Not that I want anything out of it y'understand, but a feller likes to see a good turn appreciated.

Guess who I met today? My old friend, Milton Cooper, which used to be Morris Kaufman, only he changed his name since he moved his store from Grand Street to Fifth Avenue. He told me he needed some money in his business and he went to a bank, where the president told him if he would have me endorse his note the bank would give him the money, so that's why he comes down to see me. What do you think of that for gratitude, Eddie? After all the favors I done for that feller, the minute he needs money he goes to the president of the bank, instead of first coming to me. You know what I told him? I says to him, says I, you're ungrateful. The idea of you're going to the bank president first, I says. Why didn't you come to me first, and I would let you have the money right away, if you would first have the bank president endorse your note.

What do you think of the market? The market acts nervous, don't it? Why is the market nervous, Eddie, are they afraid of something? You better sell everything except my St. Paul preferred, which I don't want to sell till it comes back to what I paid for it, if I live that long. Don't sell my Reading neither, altho maybe I got to go to Baltimore for one day, so I can't watch the market, and suppose you put in an order to sell it at 125 good for the day only. Not that I think it will jump there, but you can never tell what might happen in the market. I just want to have an order in, and with love from the family to your family, I am,

Yours,
JOE.

P.S. Why don't you give me a good tip once in a while?
P.S. I never play tips but I like to talk about them after they have made good.
P.S. If something happens in the market phone me.

Clem's Comment:

In those days there was a sideline in personally guaranteeing loans to businesses, where entrepreneurs would get their friends to effectively finance their businesses by giving a personal guarantee. It's money for nothing if the business doesn't go bust. It is like taking insurance premiums. Of course, many a friendly backer got burnt when their friend failed. It was the ruin of many a man. It was warned against in many "how to be rich" books of the time.

Here Joe says, he would have lent the friend the money if only he had got the bank to guarantee the loan and was annoyed he should suggest the deal go the other way around.

Meanwhile Joe is expressing a classic investor mistake, waiting to sell on the hope of getting even. The answer is, of course, sell when you think the stock is no longer cheap, even if it's fallen. Hold if the stock is cheap even if you are making a packet. However, many support and resistance points are determined by buying points where losers are aiming to sell at when they get back to even. It's a short term phenomenon but one that shows this illogical behaviour at work.

Savannah, Ga., July 2, 1919.

Dear Eddie:

As you can see it by the post-mark I am in Savannah which is so different from Atlantic City as buttermilk is from champain if you know what I mean. My partner has sold a bill of goods to the Enterprise Clothing company without even looking them up and first thing I know he wires me to leave my loafing and collect $1,243.85 which is overdue so long our head bookkeeper makes out the same monthly bill a year in advance at a time. So anyway I dont know what the market is doing and thats why I'm writing to you, Eddie, to find out whats what and what aint.

I wired you to sell my Southern Pacific and now I see by the papers that its 106. I suppose you sold it at 102 and something, didn't you. You wouldn't be Eddie if you didn't get me the rottenest execution. Why is it the minute I sell my stocks, no matter which they are, right away they go up. Did you ever see it fail? Next time I'm going to fool them, so when I give you an order to sell something don't do it, and then we'll see if the market goes up. Aint that a clever trick? I tell you Eddie when you play the market you get on to these new wrinkles.

Julius Feldman the architect is living here for the Spring he says, and the way that feller behaves you would think he had a commission to design the Statue of Liberty or the Woolworth Building, instead of some cheap apartment houses. He says he don't believe in the stock market. Well I answers him he aint got nothing on me, for I don't believe in it neither, the only difference being that it costs me nearly $15,000 to find it out, and he never bought a share of stock in his life. Just think Eddie what he would think of the market if he had lost as much as I have. It couldn't even be whispered, hey, Eddie!

Yours, etc.

JOE.

P.S. I ain't done so bad so far. I collected $100 on account.

P.S. When I tell you to sell some stocks, I'll tell you if I am serious or fooling.

P.S. What do you think of the market?

Clem's Comment:

Joe is getting paranoid. He thinks because he buys at the top and sells at the bottom the whole market is watching him. It can feel like this as we all close at the bottom sometimes. Our friend has lost $15,000 which is 25%-35% of his net wealth. This might be because he is being badly advised but wait – the market is random, he will get it right half the time and wrong half the time. So how come he is losing?

He is trading fast and the market in those days had a spread 2-3% wide and commissions of 1% – and remember that margin interest.

The $15,000 loss is in effect simply the costs, hidden or otherwise, of trading. Remember that 100 shares of Sumatra at $175? That's $17,500 of stock, a third to a quarter of his net worth. Buy and sell at a Bid Ask spread of 3%, with 1% commission each way, that is $875 in costs, never mind the 7% interest on the leverage. It does not take long to burn through $15,000 of capital that way.

Today people don't see the cost either and think they lose money from being wrong. In fact as they trade without skill, at random, their losses equal their costs.

Savannah, Ga., July 10, 1919.

Dear Eddie:

I am still in the South, but it aint no pleasure believe me. Getting money out of the Enterprise Clothing Company is so easy as getting passes to the opera when Gallykurtzki sings. Moe Greenbaum the proprietor has told me more fake stories in a week than the whole German Press Bureau made up during the war, which is considerable, aint it?

What do you think of the market now? Them Italians is making a terrible holler about that the Fiume thing, aint they? What do they think about it in New York? Here in Savannah they don't even know what the Fiume matter is about. One feller told me he thought it was the left over from the gas shells which the Italians dont want to clean up and which President Wilson says they got to do. Is that right? If it is, the papers certainly must be hard up to print something.

Which is the best oil stock. I want to plunge. My mind is made up that you got to make a killing if you want to make money out of Wall Street, so I think I'll make a killing by buying some oil stock which is the best of the lot? Wire me prepaid the name of the stock you recommend so I can wire you collect to buy it for me in case I like it. I want you to leave in the order I sent you to sell 50 Baldwin G. T. C. ain it? What do those initials stand for? I always thought it meant Guaranty Trust Company, but a friend of mine says they aint in the brokerage business, and that it means Gamblers Take Chances. Thats funny, and I remain,

Yours,

JOE.

P.S. If something serious happens sell all my stocks.
P.S. If my partner phones you don't tell him you heard from me. I could be dying here for all he cares. He aint wrote me a line.
P.S. Is it hard to make a killing?

Clem's Comment:

Fiume was a European flare up after the First World where a town once part of the Austro-Hungarian empire with a large Italian community was squabbled over by Italy and Yugoslavia. The Italian side was dominated by proto-fascists who would come to greatly influence Mussolini who in turn would form the basis of inspiration for the Nazi party of Germany.

Like all nervous investors with a hair trigger Joe is likely to sell the bottom of the market correction caused by this, at the time, obscure conflict.

Atlantic City, July 14, 1919.

Dear Eddie:

Well, I'm back in Atlantic City, thank goodness, and such a trip I had I wouldn't wish on my worst enemy, not even my partner. If you don't order a lower berth five weeks in advance you don't got no chance to get anything but an upper which, believe me Eddie is worse than our pressing room in the summertime, and as comfortable as a feller in a dress suit at the plumber's ball.

I see the market is strong and all the fellers what write for the newspapers is looking for a reaction. Does that mean that the market will come back again? Does my account stand even yet? If I hadn't bought that there Texas & Pacific which goes up ten points in a week you would be calling for margin again, aint it? Calling for margin is about the best thing your firm knows how to do, and they aint so bashful when it comes to charging interest neither. Between the losses you make for me and the commissions, taxes and interest your firm charges me every month I'm lucky if there is anything left. Which reminds me that this time I should give you a tip instead of your giving it to me, besides which this is a good one which yours never are. Listen Eddie, buy some Burns Bros. Coal. Its absolutely good for 200 before the end of the year. How do I know? Well if I told you who gave me this information you would hock you wife's wedding ring to get in on it.

Eddie please see what you can find out about this here Burns Coal because I want to buy a lot of it. The way my family spends money while I am away in Savannah is criminal. Yesterday my Fannie bought a sport coat she calls it on the boardwalk, which it cost $30 and nearly broke my heart to pay it when I know that Leopold Bros. sell them to the trade for $150 a dozen less 2% 10 days. My son Milton is going around with a bunch of loafers whose fathers give them more pocket money a week than I earn a year, and Milton tries to keep up with them. This morning he asked me for his allowance for November, he is drawing so far in advance. Flora is feeling much better only she wants now to go to North Carolina which makes me feel sick.

Yours,

JOE.

P.S. Send me $500 if my account and the firm can stand it.
P.S. Don't forget about Burns Coal.
P.S. Shouldn't an ice stock be better in summertime?

Clem's Comment:

Joe is getting hit by all those costs again and trading on tips. These days he could look up all possible information on Burns Coal but in 1919 information was thin on the ground. As such you can understand that gossip could be so important, yet today the urge to buy on tips is still a key feature of traders.

Atlantic City, July 25, 1919.

Dear Eddie:

Every day I see it's another million share day. That's some business your firm must be doing. How much does your firm make in commissions a day? Of course you can't tell me, and I ain't really asking you, only it must be a lot of money, hey Eddie?

What would you advise me to buy in the market just now, or would you wait until the market came down again? Everything is so high, and all the market letters I read say that the tecknikle position is getting weak. I dont know what that means but it dont sound allright so I guess I'll better wait, unless of course you know something that is A one first class high grade inside straight information about some stock that will positively go up within the next week, in which case buy me only 100 shares, because last time you had something absolutely positive, I never even saw daylight after I had bought the stock. This time dont tell me unless you are buying some yourself after you have bought my stock for me, and not before, y'understand, Eddie?

I got your wire this morning telling me that you was putting my name down on one of these here syndicates for 500 shares. Tell me something about it, I never even heard of the name. Do you think it's all right, Eddie? I suppose it aint, thats why you put me down! Do I have to put up any money in advance, or do I just sign some papers and wait for my check, if any? Is there any liability on signing any of those syndicate papers, because if there is maybe you better make it out in the name of Goodman & Gold, Inc., which is our firm name, and is incorporated by Sidney Simon, the best lawyer in the ladies ready-to-wear business.

Oh, Eddie, I nearly forgot why I wanted to write you. Tell me your honest opinion on what you think of the market, because if you say its all right to buy I want to load up, and if you dont think its the time to load up, I wont do it. If it aint the time, maybe it would be a good idea to buy "short" aint it, or is it sell short? I can never make that trick speculation out. Someday when I am in your office you can explain it to me. Let me hear from you right away because I want to do something to make expenses. It seems that when you stay in Atlantic City you pay not only for the name of the place, but for the boardwalk, the reputation, the salt water taffy, the sea air, and even the rolling chairs. If my family ever lets up on me, I will come back to New York and stay in my apartment on Lenox Avenue for the rest of my life, so help me God!

Yours, etc.,

JOE.

P.S. Give me your personal opinion on this new Syndicate.
P.S. Do you think I should sign my own name or the firms?
P.S. If it's really good, don't tell my partner anything about it.

Clem's Comment:

Looks like Joe is turning into a rogue trader. He wants to know if he should book the profit to himself or the loss to the company. Ouch! He is also getting into a syndicated deal without knowing what his liabilities will be. These days you might claim you were mis-sold but then there was no such protection.

Meanwhile he is worried that Eddie might front run his order. By doing this Eddie could buy the stock, let Joe push the price up with his stock buy, then sell himself for a fast profit. It's illegal now, but probably not back then.

Joe is also doing a trading disaster classic mistake. He thinks his wins are of his own making and his losses caused by someone else. In the market, the losses are all your own fault.

Meanwhile it seems his business partner may wake up with his business asset dissipated by Joe's reckless gambling.

Atlantic City, July 28, 1919.

Dear Eddie:

You dont have to read this letter if you dont want to, because I am sore at you and your firm, and maybe I'll say somethings you dont like to hear, so as I said before, you dont have to read it if you dont want to, but it wouldent do you or your firm any harm to hear sometimes what your customers think of you.

In the first place what is this increase in the commission business? Aint it enough that you always charge me 7½% interest without also increasing the commissions? Between those commission charges and the interest every month I got to keep on trading to pay your firm's expenses first before I even see a nickel for my own pocket.

And I aint finished with this interest business neither. I aint spoken to no fewer than six fellers here which is trading with respectable firms in Wall Street, y'understand, and not one of them is charged more than 7% and two of them pay only 6¾%. Why should your firm always be like Tiffany & Co. when it comes to interest charges?

Say, Eddie, who have you got on the floor of the Stock Exchange which executes my orders? Believe me, Eddie, no better word ever had a better meaning. Yesterday I put in an order to buy 100 Cigar Stores at 196 and I see no less than 1,000 shares sell there and I don't even get my 100. What kind of business do you call that? Moe Asher put in an order at the same price and he got his all right because his broker was attending to business while your man must have been thinking I want to buy one of the stores instead of 100 shares of the stock. If I don't get better service I'm going to transfer my account to Sachs Brothers which is closer related to me anyways.

What I got written above aint no fooling, y'understand, Eddie, only of course dont take me too serious because I was all excited when I wrote what I said in the beginning. Can't you see that I am treated a little better, Eddie, not like one of the relations, but just like an absolute stranger? Maybe that will help.

This feller Moe Asher I mentioned before is a great one for playing jokes on a feller. He just told me that he didden't buy 100 Cigar Stores at all, because he could only afford 10 shares of such a high price stock and that he paid 198. How can you tell when a feller is serious or joking? The weather here is terrible. Hoping you are the same,

Yours, etc.,
JOE.

P.S. I just got my statement and see you charge me 6¾%. I guess you knew this letter was coming.

P.S. I see Cigar Stores is down to-day. Its a good thing you didn't get it yesterday.

P.S. Buy me 100 Cigar Stores to-morrow as cheap as you can.

Clem's Comment:

The weather here is terrible. Hoping you are the same. Another classic mistake. It's not the broker who loses you money, it's the investment choices you make, or rather the lack of them. 100 shares at $196 dollars. $19,600 in stock. Even at 6 ¾% interest that's $1,323 a year in interest, or put another way, 53 ounces of Gold in 1919 or $75,000. Joe is trading in giant size for his wealth. A single position like this is roughly 33% of his net worth and costs are eating him alive. Meanwhile the broker happily gives him the rope to hang himself because all his losses are in his costs and the broker gets a fat slice of the costs.

Meanwhile Goldman Sachs, we assume, is in the wings. In 1919 would a move to the "squid" have changed his luck?

Atlantic City, Aug. 7, 1919.

Dear Eddie:

There's a feller here which calls himself Irving Black which used to be Isaac Schwartz before he made millions out of the war; and what he don't think he knows about the stock market would fill the Encyklopia Britania (did I spell it right) and the Congressional Record, and leave enough over for Webster's Unabridged Dictionary.

You know he used to be in the piece goods business, and he thinks all other businesses should be run the way he used to run his business. Even the stock market. Last week he tried some of his smart tricks on his brokers and I should like to know what they did to him. Imagine Eddie, he buys 100 Southern Pacific at 99 and when he gets the notice he looks at the newspaper and sees that his stock is down to 96, and so he writes his broker a letter something like this: Dear Sirs: I have received the 100 Southern Pacific which you bought for me, and as same is not up to standard, size and quality, I send same back to you, as I don't want it. If you don't want to give me my cash back right away I will take 100 Union Pacific for it, provided it doesn't cost me anything extra.

What do you think of that for nerve, Eddie. With Union Pacific selling about 30 points higher, and Schwartz thinks that his stockbrokers aint got no brains! Of course, I know one broker which aint got very much between his ears, his forehead and his Truly Kaufman, but we wont indulge in personalities now, hey, Eddie!

This morning I received another call for margin. That's the fourth time in the last two weeks your firm has insulted me. I suppose even if I put up 100% you would want 25% extra as a matter of habit. That margin clerk of yours aint got no shame whatever. Why don't you tell him that I'm good for anything I do? And if he wants my firm's statement, he can call up my partner any time he wants. I know some people what trades with firms that hardly want any margin at all. I guess those firms knows that there is such a thing as credit and honesty which two words your margin clerk wouldn't recognise if they was spelt out for him, and explained in eighteen different languages.

They tell me that the insiders is picking up all the cheap railroad stocks. Why is it that all the information I got to get from other people? Never do I hear a whisper from you. I could be dead and three times buried for all you care about me or my account. If I don't write you every other day I wouldn't even know I had an account. The only time I hear from your firm is when they ask for margin, and that seems to be seven times a week. Flora says you must ask your wife to come down and stay with us for a few days, but I aint given her no encouragement, all of which you can tell your wife as not.

Yours, etc.,

JOE.

P.S. If Schwartz wants to open an account with you don't take it. He's always up to something.

P.S. One of those firms which takes business on only hardly no margin all failed this morning, so I see by the paper.

P.S. Don't take serious what I said about your wife. I ain't got nothing against her. It's her husband.

Clem's Comment:

It's a hard life being a margin clerk, then and now. No one wants a margin call and many don't have funds to cover one. As such a margin call that can't be covered means the speculator must have their positions closed and crystallise the loss. In the crash of 2008 many spread betting and CFD companies took huge losses when clients simply couldn't cover their losses. Undoubtedly this is what caused the companies who were easy on margins in 1919 to go bust.

Every gambler loves a bookie when he wants credit and hates him when he has to pay up. Trading is not investing, it is gambling and the outcomes are the same.

Of course in the US there were few places to gamble and so Wall Street became the casino as it remains today.

Atlantic City, Aug. 10, 1919.

Dear Eddie:

What's the matter with you fellers there in New York, aint you got enough excitement with the war, and the riots, and the strikes, and everything without putting the market up and down so fast it must give a feller which is close to the tape absolute heart failure. God knows the evening newspapers gives me nervous headaches.

Whats the matter anyways. I guess the fellers which is running the market aint made their mind up yet which way they want it to go. I hope they decide soon, and I don't care which way neither so long as I don't figure up profits one day, and losses the next, that is — on paper. Believe me, I wouldn't sell or buy in this kind of a market. Not on your life. This is the kind of a market you brokers make so much in commissions you should be ashamed to charge any interest at all, but I never heard of Wall Street houses giving anything away. I suppose when I get my statement for the month it will be 7½% same as before. I'll bet you couldn't find me another house which charges more, while maybe 99% charges less.

Listen Eddie, how does my account stand now? Am I long or short. Since I left all my trading in your hands I never know whether I bought or sold or whether I should eat lunch at the Traymore or Childs. Last week I made a terrible mistake. Remember you told me I should buy Rubber because something is doing quick for 30 points sure, and I told you to go ahead, so when I seen it go up 10 points I took Flora and Milton and Fannie to the Blenheim for the finest dinner we ever ate at $2.50 a head, and when I received your notice in the morning I seen you was short. Why did you change your mind when you was once right. You don't suppose I'm going to let you put that loss on Rubber in my account after you told me you was buying it? Not even if I am your uncle there are certain liberties you cant take with me, no sir!

Has my partner called you up lately? He wants to know if the joint account is making or losing money. If he asks you tell him it makes no never mind as he don't let me know how much he draws for expenses while I am away, but maybe you shouldn't mix between partners, and I remain,

Yours, etc.,

JOE.

P.S. Send me a check for $10 you owe me for the dinner I spent.

P.S. What do you hear on So. Pac.? My wife has some of the convertible 5s.

P.S. Don't trade any more for my account unless you make profits. Charge somebody else with the losses.

Clem's Comment:

Charge someone else with the losses. It sounds like a joke of course but brokers have been known to guarantee profits. Of course bad things then happen. It is also illegal but that didn't stop Japanese brokers making such profits in the boom years. They did of course come unstuck.

Of course these days mis-selling amounts to the same thing. Is the regulator clawing back any gains from people who bought mis-sold products that made them profits? So passing losses on risk taking to other people is not so ridiculous after all. Then of course there is QE, yet another scheme to pass losses from risky gamblers on to careful savers.

Hold on a minute, did Eddie long rubber and pretend Joe had shorted it? Is Eddie actually charging Joe for his losses, by making a bug and a short sale of a stock and booking the profit to his account and the loss to Joe? No, that could never happen . . .

Atlantic City, Aug. 20, 1919.

Dear Eddie:

Eddie this is a great place if I say so myself. Yesterday I was sitting in your branch office here and a feller comes in and without any show at all he gives a order to buy a thousand General Motors which he wants to put away and pay for. I suppose you know that means an outlay of $215,000 or can't you figure that high. Today this here same feller comes back and buys another thousand shares and again he pays for it, so I looks up and takes notice. Says I to myself this here feller must be Vanderbilt or Morgan or Rockefeller to be able to cut into his bank account without making a hole in it. Imagine my surprise Eddie when I ask the manager for his name and his business and he tells me that this feller has been buying stocks like this all season, and he pays right out for them too, and what's more Eddie, this feller is the guy what has the rolling chair privilege at Atlantic City. Of course when I heard that I wasn't surprised none at all, for I must have paid that guy several thousand dollars for my family alone and we've only been here three weeks.

Eddie there certainly is some bunch of people here. It seems like the whole white goods trade from St. Louis and the enter clothing trade from Cleveland is stopping at one hotel. You know which hotel I mean and I don't have to mention any names altho maybe I could get a nice room there for nothing if I mentioned the name and you published this letter. Advertising is a great thing aint it? I'll say it is.

Eddie if you ever owe anybody any money or youre out with somebody else's wife, or you have robbed a bank, or youve done anything else that you dont want nobody to see you, for heavens sake dont go to Atlantic City. The first day I was here and I take a walk on this here boardwalk and the only people I didn't meet I never knew. Flora and me cant walk five steps without bumping into some relation or friend. Honest would you believe me it takes us two hours to walk from the Traymore to the Breakers. Not that I am living at either place y'understand. The first place is too expensive and the other place I would meet all my wife's relations, and as I aint exactly keen about either the best I can do is Mrs. Epstein's boarding house where we get good home cooking and clean towels every other day.

Just because I aint go no stocks now Eddie is no reason why you shouldn't give me some inside information sometimes so don't be stingy and when something good comes along count me in. Give me a flash when you get a good tip, maybe I can swing some business your way. If I buy some stock first and my friend comes in after me and buy some more it puts the stock up, aint it and then you can sell me out right away. Flora and Fannie and Irving send their regards to you and your family. Has you wife still got roomatism, and oblige,

Yours, etc.,
JOE.

P.S. Buy me some good stock that will go up next week. I can't never seem to make my expenses here.

P.S. Suppose you open an account in my wife's name, so when a stock is good and goes up you can put it in her account instead of the joint account I have with my partner.

P.S. Don't tell my partner about this wife's account business. He might get sore.

Clem's Comment:

Denial, anger, bargaining and finally grief. This is the cycle of loss. Joe is in bargaining mode. He also wants some of that front running action. If the client wants to buy big, the unethical/illegal trading broker buys first. The client pushes the market up and the broker takes his quick profit. Anybody between the client and the market can play this dirty trick and it's been illegal for some time. However it wasn't illegal in 1919. Not much was.

Atlantic City, Aug. 29, 1919.

Dear Eddie:

I suppose my account is positively cleaned out, aint it, after what I seen in the papers about the market going way down and everything, but why diddent you call for more margin, instead of just selling me out like any other customer? Not that I should have sent you more margin, because you know how my finances are at this time with Flora having seven operations per month and Milton running up more bills in a week than I would spend on myself in six years, and my Fannie, she's a good girl but she should have a Father which owns Altman, Tiffany and Sherrys to satisfy her tastes. It seems that the ladies ready to wear business was invented so that the profits should be spent on a man's family!

Is it a good time to go short? I see that Pres. Wilson is going after all the profiteers, which is a good business but he should take my advice and go after the Wall Street brokers first, because the interest they charge a feller every month is eating my heart out. And your firm aint no exception neither. I should say it the other way, maybe your firm leads the list. But getting back to the market, I think all the stocks is going way down, so you should sell something for me, and if it goes way down, and you think I should buy it back, let me know and I will give you instructions. I aint going to let you use your own judgment any more, since you do nothing but make explanations instead of profits.

I'm glad I aint the only feller which was caught on the wrong side of the market last week. Abe Hirshman came here from Saint Louis last week and was so busy buying children's dresses for his department store, he diddent have time to look at the market, so when I seen him last night he comes up and tells me how much money he made on a bill of goods he bought cheap and resold right away, and offers to buy me a dinner, so I diddent have the heart to accept when I know his wife has been running around the hotel like crazy waving telegrams calling for margin, and not knowing what to do. Afterwards he told me he lost enough money to buy another department store, and he is through with the market for good, so help him God!

Well, Eddie, let me know what you think of things, and dont do anything until I advise you as I wont be responsible. Buy them when they're cheap and sell them when they're dear. Thats the only way to make money in Wall Street, aint it? Only when is a feller to know when is when? Thats the secret J. P. Morgan wouldnt give up for a million dollars, hey, Eddie.

Come down to see us soon, only let me know in advance so Flora can tell the cook to make noodle soup.

Yours, etc.,
JOE.

P.S. Can't you do something to charge me less interest?
P.S. Don't forget to let me know whether I should go short or long.
P.S. If your wife comes with you, let me know so we can have strudel, too.

Clem's Comment:

Buy them when they're cheap and sell them when they're dear. Only when is a feller to know when is when?

Well, it's not too tricky. When the P/E is below 12, and the dividend is above 3% and directors are buying big chunks of their own stock, chances are a feller should look closely at the company.

But Joe isn't looking for a value investment, he is looking to make money now. There was no chance then as there is no chance now. There is no such thing as a free lunch, noodle or otherwise.

Atlantic City, N. J., Sept. 5, 1919.

Dear Eddie:

Its about time the market did something, aint it, after all the dull times they is having in Wall Street. I don't know just what is doing, only the evening papers here say the market aint doing nothing at all, and here you have me loaded up to my neck with stocks which I can't get out of if they went up even 20 points and the interest I am paying could pay for a week's board for my family here, and the prices they're charging don't make that no piker amount neither.

Why don't you do something for me. Buy something or maybe it should be better to sell something. What do you think? I hear the labor troubles is terrible all over the country and that stocks will go down. Shouldn't I sell everything I got and maybe I'll get it back cheaper. Then again maybe the market has already discounted all the bad news and it would be better for me to average. This averaging business is great stuff, only it dont get you no where except maybe the poor house.

That was a great strike you had in New York when the subways and street cars wouldn't run, and everybody had to walk, unless they could afford a taxi. Milton Stein which was in New York last week says he couldn't hire a taxi unless he assigned his will in advance, the prices they wanted was something terrible. Only I know Milton, and he would rather walk his shoeleather off twice than pay those robbers a nickel over the regular fare. He says he met you on Broadway, also walking down. What's the matter Eddie, aint you made enough out of my account alone to buy a automobile, or are you so close, everytime you let go a quarter the eagle on it chokes to death? Milton told me you are a great one in doping out things on the stock market. He says you thought maybe Endicott Johnson would go up because all the people had to walk and would wear out a lot of shoe leather. Then he says you said maybe Wilson & Co. or maybe Indian Packing or Allied Packing or National Biscuit or some of the other food stocks should go up because people would get such a appetite from walking. And then he says you said maybe Cigar Stores and Tobacco Products and America Sumatra should go up because people would smoke more when they walk which they couldn't do if they ride in the trains, but Eddie, when Milton told me you said maybe United Drug should go up because the people walking in the rain would all catch colds and have to take medicine, I throwed up my hands and decided to transfer my account because I wouldnt have my money with a house which employs lunatics. Hoping your wife is the same I am,

Yours, etc.,

JOE.

P.S. Are you coming to see us soon? Flora has a new dress she wants to show off.

P.S. Don't do anything in my account like you told Milton.

P.S. I notice all the stocks you thought would go up has gone down so much they wouldn't come back if we had strikes on the street cars every day.

Clem's Comment:

Ah, narrative, what would the market do without it? These days the market goes up because bad news is good news. Bad news means more QE so stocks rally. Then we have good news and stocks go up because good news is good for stocks. You can't have it both ways but if you write headlines you can.

The market is mainly random so it can go up for no reason at all, but "Market rockets on probabilistic noise" will never be a headline.

Atlantic City, N. J., Sept. 10, 1919.

Dear Eddie:

I got a peculiar feeling which don't make me feel all right at all, because I'm so nervous I can't sleep. I dream about the market all night long because I'm short of Keystone Tire since 50 and when it went to 60 I sold some more, and now it's 68 and a friend of mine which is related to a member of the crowd which they say is putting it up says it will reach 200 sure in sixty days. I never knew what it meant to be short of the market. Its such a rotten feeling you can't describe it. Now when I buy something and it costs $50 a share, I aint worried none at all if it should go down because the most I can lose is 50 points, but when you sell something short at 50, it can just as well go to 500 there aint no limit, and thats the rotten feeling I have. Every night I dream the stock opens up 100 points and I must ask Flora to sell all her jewelry, which God knows I'd rather do anything else in the world. You know her temper, right or wrong.

Well, Eddie, old top, I might as well be jolly, as not, for whats the use to be all the time thinking about a stock like Keystone, and anyway I dont think it will run away, do you? But leaving the stock market aside, how's everything by you? You know, since I came down here and everybody I know seems to be making piles of money I've become the biggest liar you ever saw. In order to keep up with the bunch I got to say I trade in thousands of shares I never even seen at all. The funny part of it is that my imagination is becoming so real I get a stomach ache every time I think of my actual bank balance. Anyways I got one consoltion. Maybe my neighbours is also trying to kid me in which case the biggest liar is the worst off, aint it?

Do you think I should cover my Keystone now or wait until something happens? Everybody says it aint worth the paper its printed on, but it keeps right on going up. Its just like the argument we have home every day about our cook. Flora keeps on telling me she's absolutely honest, and I keep on telling Flora the cook's positively honest, but things keep on missing every day. Of course, there isnt exactly a resemblance between our cook and Keystone, but I'm certain of one thing. Neither is worth what they're getting.

Is there much doing in the market these days other than Keystone. Really I'm a little worried about that stock but then you cant blame me. Well, lets forget about it for a couple of days, I want to get the stock out of my mind anyway and I suppose youre sick hearing about my troubles, which I dont blame you none, but suppose you were out nearly $10,000, hey Eddie, then you wouldn't be so chipper neither. Remember me to the family, and dont tell nobody nothing about this Keystone business, because its none of their affairs.

Yours, etc.,

JOE.

P.S. See what you can find out about Keystone.
P.S. I only want some bad news. I hear all the good news down here.
P.S. Don't even tell your wife about this Keystone business.

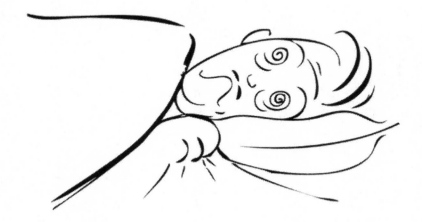

Clem's Comment:

As I write there are quite a few worthless stocks worth hundreds of million in London. One just shot up 60% today. I'm not short, but it would be logical to be short of such rubbish. However you can't beat a fraud on its own terms. You have to let it run its course.

Now imagine this. A stock is 400p or $400 a share. It's a brilliant fraud. Everyone loves it. Bad news strikes. It falls from 400 to 10. The company is effectively dead. You made 97.5%.

Instead you wait until its effectively dead and sell it at 10 and it goes bust. You make 100%. You didn't need a 390 point fall to make 97.5%.

I don't recommend you do this at all, but you see the effect of the maths.

In any event when you are short you have an unlimited downside and a limited upside. That's a hard asymmetry.

What is worse, bubbles and frauds and bubble frauds go up massively, 2, 5, 10, 30 times. Now leverage that up 10 times.

Boooom! This is how you go broke fast.

Atlantic City, N. J., Sept. 18, 1919.

Dear Eddie:

I dont want to stay here any more, because prices is going up every day, and my account with you aint making any money, so the combination should send me to the poor house right away quick.

First, my Fannie is giving me the jumps the way she's going around with Simon Jaffe who is a gambler and a bum and no good for anything. You know his father don't you, Isidore Jaffe of Jaffe Brothers which go through bankruptcy so regular they got their legal forms prepared three years in advance? Anyway this Jaffe feller is hanging around and staying to dinner and Fannie likes him too, that's the rotten part of it because I know if something comes of it, I should be supporting them for the rest of their life, whereas take for instance Sidney Kirschbaum, whose father is Abe Kirschbaum of Kirschbaum & Kahn, very rich bankers, I don't need to tell you about them, well my Fannie don't want nothing to do with him, and he's crazy about her, and wants to buy her the Pennsylvania Railroad and the Woolworth Building if she wants it. Aint girls the limit?

Then Milton is spending so much money all the time he thinks his father is paying teller at a bank. I aint been giving him any money at all lately but when the first of the month came around I received enough bills to start a bonfire. He can do more with other people's money than anybody I ever seen so I think I'll send him up to your office so you can give him a job. He should be right at home there, hey Eddie!

Say, thats some Convention the bankers is holding down here! From the newspapers I seen that all the big fellers from Wall Street is here talking over what's to be done to the stock market, aint it. Last night I pulled a good one. I was in the lobby of the Traymore with Louis Breslau talking about old times when we was both working in the cutting room for Samstag Bros. when all of sudden he says do I know whose that talking over in the corner, so I says no, and he says they're the fellers which has been putting Keystone up and down, and maybe they're fixing something for next week, so I quickly got a bell boy to go over and find out what they're talking about and slipped him a dollar so he wouldn't find out and tell somebody else. Well, Eddie, I found out what they were talking about. When the bell boy came back all smiles like Steeplechase I felt myself growing richer by the minute and when I asked him did he hear and he said yes, I felt like kissing him, but imagine my surprise when I asks him what were they talking about, and he says "Boss, they was talking about the ladies!"

Maybe you can tie it, but you can't beat it.

Send me some of those special cigars you give to customers. The prices they charge for cigars here is not only criminal, its heart breaking.

Yours, etc.

JOE.

P.S. Let me know what stocks Kirschbaum & Kahn is interested in. Maybe I can get Fannie to find out something for me from young Sidney.

P.S. 50-50 on anything good what comes out of it.

P.S. Don't forget the cigars. If you make some money in the market for me, I'll pay you back.

Clem's Comment:

Maybe you can tie it, but you can't beat it.

Gambling has been called "better than sex" but clearly the stock market isn't all gambling.

To think that in those days groups of people would manipulate prices of stocks.

It couldn't happen now!

Sadly it happens every day even in the most highly regulated of markets.

Bear in mind however they do it to lure in Joe and his kind. These games are to catch the Joes of this world, which in the old days would be called "degenerate gamblers." You know what Joe likes and so do they. Don't buy the kind of action Joe buys. If you don't you won't go far wrong. Invest instead.

Boston, Mass., Oct. 2, 1919.

Dear Eddie:

Well, Eddie, as you can see by the date line I am in Boston, which, believe me, is no place to be when the market is closed, because you can't get any information from the brokers here. Not that they would know anything even if I asked them, y'understand, but you always feel like asking them something about stocks, and what they think of market. I met one feller here today who is in the Wall Street section, only they call it Milk Street here, which is a funny name for a street which has only brokers' offices. They must milk the people here like they do in New York, hey, Eddie?

They got the funniest streets here you ever saw. This morning I was walking on Summer street and the first thing you know I was on Winter street. How quick the seasons change in Boston. I wonder if everything goes quick like this in Boston. They tell me the copper stocks is going up because Tom Lawson, which is King up here, says so. Is that right, Eddie, and have you heard the like in New York? Buy me some of those copper stocks if you dope is right, because I want to make a killing. Flora and I motored up here from Atlantic City, and the only thing we didn't have on the road was the measles. Five punctures and two blow-outs, and when I needed some new tubes and tires they must have thought I was Morgan or Vanderbilt, the prices they charged me. Believe me, Eddie, this here car of mine is going back on the boat. I ain't going to drive that flivver back to New York.

I wouldn't have come up here to this town, only my partner wires me to see Kaplan & Lefkowitz, who is starting in business for themselves, and maybe we can get a nice order. The way that partner of mine sends me all over the country is a shame. And he always looks at my expense bill with a magnifying glass. Last time I took a trip to Cleveland and I took my family along, and I only charged up their railroad fare and didn't make any mention of hotel bills or anything, and he kicks about it. What do you know about that, and the last time he went away for the firm he only went to Philadelphia and the bill he put in could have taken care of President Wilson, his wife and seventeen secretaries for a month. The nerve of him! Dont tell him I am sore about this, Eddie, because it would only make us get into an argument, which is all we really do anyway.

I didn't ask you anything about the market, Eddie, because I know you are busy, very busy, but I wish you could get some time to tell me what you think of Steel, So. Pac., Reading and General Electric. I don't want to know much. Just let me know what dividend they have paid since they is in business and the high and low.

Yours, etc.,
JOE.

P.S. Also get me some up-to-the-minute statistics on National Biscuit, and Sinclair Oil.

P.S. Do you know somethings about Texas Co., Corn Products, California Petroleum, and Cigar Stores?

P.S. If it aint asking too much, tell me which do you like better for a quick profit? Either Rock Island, Southern Railway, and Baldwin or Midvale, National Enameling, and Studebacker? Also why?

Clem's Comment:

Of course if Joe had ADVFN he would be in great shape. Meanwhile imagine staking 20% of your net worth on a stock that had little or no information about it, in a market rife with insider trading, manipulation and thievery. There were no stock charts as such, unless you kept the data yourself and drew it by hand. The only price was one coming down a ticker tape. The order you sent to buy or sell was by telegraph and heaven knew when and at what price you got execution at.

And still they played.

You mustn't play for the same reasons.

Atlantic City, N. J., Oct. 6, 1919.

Dear Eddie:

For the second time I must ask you to explain to me what G. T. C. stands for because I have been trying to buy it all week but the feller which runs your branch office down here says its very inactive and hard to get quotations on. But I don't like the tone of voice he uses when he talks to me. Something tells me in my bones there's a skeleton in the cupboard somewhere.

I'll tell you how I became interested in this here G. T. C. stock only don't breathe a word about it. Last week Jesse Livermore comes in to your office here and your customer's man pointed him out to me, so I followed him all around Atlantic City for two days without him giving anybody an order to neither buy or sell. But last Tuesday I followed him into the office of Spencer, Rushmore and Vanderpool, which certainly does a nice business with high class people like I never see in your office, and he writes out an order to buy 5,000 shares of a stock. I know it was 5,000 shares because I was standing right next to him pretending to write out a order myself. Imagine Eddie my doing business with that silk stocking firm! They would never take my account if it was worth a million dollars unless I changed my name, hey Eddie? Anyway he tried to cover up the name of the stock but I was too quick for him and saw the name. It was G. T. C. but when I looked for it in the morning paper I didn't see it quoted, and I didn't want to ask somebody what it was because that would give it away. So I rushed over to your office and put in an order for 100 shares at the market. I didn't get it, and ain't got it yet. What's the matter with those boobs, don't they know what stock it is? All they say is they ain't got it yet but the broker is trying to buy it carefully. I told him never mind that broker being so careful, he should get me the stock and be done with it.

It's the funniest thing. Since that day I put in the order for my 100 G.T.C. and didn't get it, every time I come in your office somebody has always just told a good joke about something because they're all laughing tears like perspiration, and I ain't in on it.

Well, I must close now Eddie as Flora is waiting for me to take her to dinner. She says we must walk in the dining room together, and it ain't nice for me to sit down first before she and the children come in. Ain't it remarkable how fussy they get if its only a little ways from Lenox Avenue?

Yours, etc.,

JOE.

P.S. I just got an idea. I'll fool everybody and make my order on that 100 G. T. C. good till canceled.

P.S. I just phoned the order in but the clerk is got the hikkups or something. He said he entered 100 G. T. C. G. T. C.

P.S. I guess the joke's on me, ain't it?

Clem's Comment:

Good till cancelled. That is still an order type now and there are plenty of others, like fill or kill, market order, limit order etc. These days there are tranche orders and iceberg orders . . . The take away is, investing and especially trading is a skill game, don't play it hard if you don't know the rules and don't have the tools.

If you do you will lose your shirt.

Today Joe would be called a muppet. Goldman Sach got caught with one of its men calling its clients muppets, but Goldman didn't come up with the phrase.

In 1919 you were a chump. In 2013 you might be a muppet. The result is the same, losses. Losses driven solely by the cost of trading and randomness.

It isn't easy being green and it's hard to get in the black, if you're a muppet.

On Board the Special Train, Oct. 10.

Dear Eddie:

I'm on the train going to St. Louis, where they are holding the Investment Bankers Convention, so maybe you must right away ask me why I should go to a Bankers Convention when I am nearly retiring from the ladies ready to wear business but when I explain to you that we are carrying a big line of credit with the Economy National Bank, and that Lou Klinger which is Vice President, asked me to come along with him, maybe you will understand. Of course everything is free and don't cost me nothing, which is also another reason, and is maybe the best reason, hey Eddie.

Say, this is some swell train. They got all compartments. I never seen such exclusiveness in my life. If you want to talk to another feller on the same train you must got to have your card sent in by the porter. That's the way they do it on a special train.

You know Eddie, I think this Special train business is all bunk. We just went into dinner and I thought maybe prices on the bill of fare would be reduced some because its a special train, but I didnt see anything reduced none at all. So I guess its a special train because everything is higher than usual instead of lower, like I always thought it was when I was in active business and we had specials every time we wanted to clean out a poor seller.

I just had a serious talk with some of the bankers on the train, and I'm worried about the stocks you are carrying for me. I think you better sell them out because they all said financial conditions aint all right. They said the reserves aint up to what they ought to be, so I thought I would say something to let them know I was interested, so I said quick like a flash "Why dont you people hire some men from the National Guard if you aint satisfied with the Reserves" and the look they gave me, Eddie, makes me feel as if something I said wasn't right.

Will write you more when I get to St. Louis if I get time between visiting all my wife's sisters relations. Be good.

Yours, etc.,
JOE.

P.S. There wasn't a good pinochle game all day.
P.S. Lou Klinger just told me he didn't buy that small bank he was dikkering about.
P.S. I just told him as long as he didn't buy it, he shouldn't have been a piker and said he didn't buy the Guaranty Trust Company, or the National City Bank.

Clem's Comment:

Investment bankers in 1919 . . . Travelling like kings, their capital reserves weak . . . has anything changed at all in 94 years???

St. Louis, Oct. 22.

Dear Eddie:

Well, here I am in the City which made Bevo famous, and I certainly am having a fine time. I just had the finest afternoon at somebody's elses expenses I ever had, and besides won $15 betting on a ball game. I took your advice, Eddie, and went to see your friends in the brokerage business here. Mark and Louis is the two nicest boys I ever met in the brokerage business in St. Louis. Of course I aint met anybody else yet, but just the same I like them. They look honest which is more than some brokers I know in New York look.

They treated me swell too. Lunch at their Club, and then for a automobile ride, and say Eddie we covered some ground! First we saw a baseball game, and then we ran into a bicycle race. We left there are bumped into a regular football game, and afterwards passed by a tennis match. Honest the way those fellers took me from one thing to another I thought they must be in the sporting goods business instead of what they tell me they handle stocks and sometimes bonds.

The boys asked me a lot of questions about your firm which I couldn't answer because I told them I'm only a customer and not a partner, and that furthermore I am a relations of yours, Eddie, which gives me even a worse chance to know something than an outside stranger. You know what I mean.

Just the same I like the boys very much because they give me such a good time. Of course I would like them also even if they wouldn't pay for everything. I don't mind spending something now and then. You know me, Eddie, but its nice just the same when you're being treated right and left. Mark asked me to sleep at his house tonight, so I accepted right away because some of his relatives do a big business with our biggest competitors in New York, and maybe if I meet them around a table of pinochle I can swing some orders my way. Of course I'm not here on business, but that don't say I shouldn't take advantage of opportunities, hey Eddie! Whats that Shakespeare once said — "If opportunity knocks on the door, don't treat him like a book agent."

And I remain,

Yours, etc.,

JOE.

P.S. Tell my partner, if he should phone you, that I am working very hard for our business.

P.S. Don't tell him I'm being treated so much. I want to put in a big expense account.

P.S. I ain't been to no convention speeches yet because I ain't felt sleepy during the day.

Clem's Comment:

Broker's hospitality is not what it used to be, but if you are a big customer like Joe then you will get it. However, it's not free. Remember, Joe's losses are equal to his costs and he appears to be down the equivalent of 1,000 ounces of gold ($25,000). That's over a million, a million of costs. Now imagine there are no rules for front running and you are free to gull such a muppet. Then a broker might be very keen, just like any casino owner, to compo you to the skies.

St. Louis, Oct. 24, 1919.

Dear Eddie:

Well, Eddie, this is Sunday and I am having the time of my life, only don't tell your wife about it, because she sees my Flora every Tuesday afternoon at the Kaffee Klatch, and maybe I would get a telegram to come back right away. Anyway Flora can't kick because I am saying hallo to all of her relations which lives here, and telling them what a good cook she was.

They certainly have made a bunch of money out of the war in this City. Mark took me up to the Club this afternoon and the way they throw the long green away you'd think the Mint moved here from Philadelphia. The biggest industry in this City is eight handed poker. Everybody does it. I saw at the Club ten games going on, with no limits neither. One of the fellers says "Stick around and you'll see a spectacular pot" so I stuck, and a feller which looked as if he hadnt shaved since McKinley died took in $1,500 on two small pairs. Can you imagine what he would of won on four aces? Of course I dont know much about poker, because as you know pinochle is more in my line, and it takes more brains to play auction, don't you think so, Eddie?

But Eddie, I'll tell the world one thing. Poker and pinochle players in St. Louis aint no different from New York. They all wear the same silk shirts, smoke the same cigars, and tell the same stories. Of course you mustn't ask me to write you some of them now, but some day when the market is dull, I'll tell you one that made me look foolish for the rest of the day.

Cant you wire me something whats absolutely good in the market, because I want to show these fellers I got some first class inside information. I told them your house was the largest in Wall Street and did all the big business on the Stock Exchange. They should know the truth!

Well Eddie, I'll close now as maybe I'll be invited to join one of the poker games, and I must got to figure out my bank balance to see how much I can lose and leave enough margin to send you in case stocks go down, and I am always

Yours respectively,

JOE.

P.S. Why dont your firm bring out a new Syndicate and sell it all in St. Louis. They got so much money they'll buy Confederate money, which aint no worse than some stocks your firm has issued lately.

P.S. Lou Klinger took me to one of the Conventions last night, but I fell asleep.

P.S. Phone my partner I must stay here all week because I'm so terrible busy.

Clem's Comment:

Buy confederate money in 1919? Buy Iraqi Saddam Dinar in 2010!

Joe of course wants to run with the crowd, he is impressed by them and wants to emulate them. Following the crowd is never, ever a good idea in the market. These days it's called making a "crowded trade." That's sounds better than following the herd or being a sheep. However the story is the same and it doesn't end well.

St. Louis, Nov. 20, 1919.

Dear Eddie:

I guess I dont care for St. Louis so terrible much. I lost nearly $2,000 playing poker Last Sunday at Mark's Club. You know Eddie playing poker for high stakes aint so exciting as the Stock market but you lose it much faster. I also thought that pinochle was the only game where you talk for the next two weeks about the hand you might have made. Well, last Sunday a feller called Moe Green raised everybody on three Jacks, and finally when the pot was nearly $1,200 to the good one feller stands pat, and Moe Green gets frightened and drops out. When the other feller finally shows that he's got only a pair of nines and rakes in all the money in the world, this Moe Green goes into hysterics, and aint recovered yet. They say he'll never be the same.

Say Eddie, you know Lou Klinger, Vice-President of the Economy National Bank, which invited me to the Convention and took me in his Special train and everything. Anyway he played poker with us and he won most of the money I lost. Even that aint so bad, but when we was leaving the Club he says he don't like the way I am gambling my money away, and he must watch our credit closer, and maybe they got to call our loan at the bank. Aint that the nerve! I wonder what his bank would do if I had won the $2,000 and he had lost it? You're always good at figuring out puzzles so let me know the answer.

My office just forwarded me last months statement and I see you are still charging me 7 per cent. Don't your firm know that money aint so tight anymore and that it is now much easier, or don't you people read the newspapers? The least you can do is to reduce it to 6¾ per cent which is all Sam Miller is paying at Kirschbaum & Kahnm, besides which that is a fine first class banking house, and it helps your credit to have a account with them. All of which is just a hint and I hope you have sense enough to take it.

The weather here is very windy. Hoping youre the same, believe me,

Yours, etc.,

JOE.

P.S. Do you got any bull information on Steel. Send me a favorable statement.
P.S. Wire me if you think Steel will go higher, also if the insiders think its going up.
P.S. If all the dope looks O.K. sell for me short 500 Steel at the market.

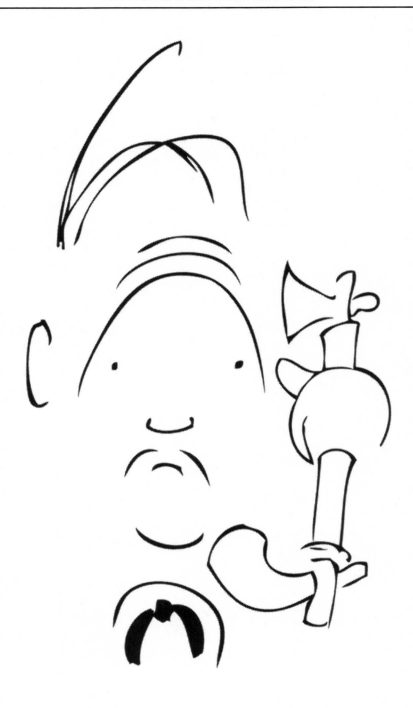

Clem's Comment:

Well we are not surprised. So was the friendly banker actually taking Joe along to sharp him at poker? Once again there is no free lunch. I once met an old poker player, of some standing in real high stakes poker. This was a world class player. It was when online poker had just started. I asked him how he was doing. He said he was losing money. I asked him why he thought that was. He said he didn't know. I asked him what would happen if all the other players were just one person with all the hands. The poor old guy nearly had a heart attack on the spot.

Money attracts all the wrong elements. Always be on guard. Poker is not Pinochle. Trading is not investing. Stocks are not CFDs. Options are not shares.

Buy cheap shares and hold them until they are not cheap. Leave the rest to the gamblers.

Atlantic City, N. J., Nov. 23, 1919.

Dear Eddie:

Aint it a wild market we're having, and stocks like General Motors going up 30 points one day and down 15 points the next. Why is it I never hear from you a word about those kind of stocks. Not that I would touch it, understand, because what happened to a friend of mine here last week is the biggest crime ever committed on the Stock Exchange. You know Louis Kafka, don't you, which owns a dry goods store in Rochester, and paid 85 cents on the dollar last time business was bad? Well, he got a tip on this here General Motors at 330 and he didn't play it so when it got to 350 was he sore? I'll say so. Anyways it goes higher and he thinks maybe he should sell short, so he goes short at 355 and that same day the stock closes at 360. That night he gets worried and can't sleep because somebody has told him it will go to 500 sure, he puts in an order to cover his stock and buy another 100 to make up the loss. He buys it at 390, and he thinks he'll protect himself by stopping it at 380, and inside of 15 minutes it goes back to 375 and he is sold out. His family don't think he'll ever be the same.

Well, what's new by you? Is there anything doing at all? Isnt there some Syndicate I can make some money out of? The last Syndicate you put me in was all right, and the check for the profits was all right, too, but the stock which you said I must take and put away aint so all right at all. Remember I asked you when you said I should subscribe whether there was any strings to the stock, and you said none at all, only it wouldnt be the right thing to do to sell it right away so I held it, and it hasn't stopped going down. If I didnt sell, somebody else did. Who was it? They should put people like that in jail, I say. If people want to go in syndicates, they shouldn't sell out right away. They must show that they got confidence in the people whats bringing the stock out.

We had a fine game of auction last night. Louise Kafka, while he aint exactly all right because of the Gen. Motors murder, still managed to make two 450 hands, both spades, in half hour, and felt a little better afterwards. Ike Stern from Albany sat in for a couple of hands. He aint lost none of his ability, let me tell you. They say he's got a son which can play even better than him. Why don't you come down soon, and play a little with us? The air is fine this time of the year, and you can walk the whole boardwalk instead of paying those thieves which own the roller chairs for every little trip you want to make. I think we'll move to a better hotel next week. The stationery here aint swell enough and our friends think we are living in a cheap boarding house, and whats more, theyre right, too.

Yours, etc.,
JOE.

P.S. If you know something like General Motors which should go up 30 points like nothing, buy me some.

P.S. About that last Syndicate, I sold my stock through another house, so I really ain't got a loss but a profit. You ain't mad, are you Eddie?

P.S. If you come down bring some new chips. Mine are wearing.

Clem's Comment:

Stop losses and volatility don't go together. Then add random trading and sprinkle with trying to "get even with the market thinking" and the outcome is . . . still random, minus costs.

In this case the degenerate trader blew himself up.

Hint: never, ever, EVER have a position that spoils your sleep. This is your subconscious mind telling you that you are gambling and have taken on too much risk.

Close those positions now. Only have ones that do not worry you. You won't get rich quick, but you won't get poor fast either.

If you trade/invest like that, guess what. You won't sleep and you won't get rich quick either but you risk getting poor fast.

So why do it at all?

Because investing is a way to get wealthy slow.

Do you know any other ways to do that?

New York, Nov. 26, 1919.

Dear Eddie:

I just heard from Flora that you must got to go away for a vacation so as in order to get away from the stock market, so I thought I should right away sit down and write you a few lines to tell you what's been doing in the stock market. You know, just to keep you informed so you won't be a boob when you return. That's me, Eddie, always looking out for your interest, even if you don't look out for mine, which by the way was 7½% last month!

I dropped into your office this morning Eddie but they're aint much doing since I came back from my vacation at Atlantic City. Nothing exciting doing at all. Of course Republic Steel went up 13 points in 13 minutes, but nobody had none, so nobody was specially interested. But you should have seen the excitement when Marine common went up a ¼! Say Eddie, you must have loaded up the whole office with that stock. How is it you didn't stick me with some, or was it a mistake?

Say Eddie, when you answer me this letter, let me know for what reason you employ a civil engineer to make pictures in your office. I didn't know it was a art studio. When I came in this morning I seen him drawing figures with a compass and a ruler, which looks just like either the Rocky Mountains or a weather report. Your assistant very kindly told me it was a chart which could tell you at a glance just what U.S. Steel was going to do next Wednesday at quarter past eleven. Its just like fortune telling, he told me. You just look at the lines and right away you make a killing. Well, thats something else I learned today. Tonight Im going to buy a compass and ruler for myself, and make some of this here easy money.

Best regards from the family, and they want me to tell you to behave yourself. What does that mean Eddie, don't they trust you away from home at all? Then I aint the only one aint I? So long. Over the river.

Yours, etc.,

JOE.

P.S. I guess that map business aint so easy. The civil engineeer asked me for a loan of $1, so he could eat lunch.

P.S. What do you think of Bessie B? The stock, I mean, not who you mean.

P.S. I think shes a bad actor. I mean the girl, not the stock.

Clem's Comment:

Why aren't stock chartists rich? Why aren't stock tipsters rich? They can't be very good if they aren't well off. That is most likely true. So it's not a bad place to start. Is the guy with the advice well off?

These days you can also follow his past advice and see how well he did.

Maybe you should close this book and do your "due dil" now. I wonder what Joe would have thought "due dil" meant? He would probably think it was a salad, eh Eddie?

New York, Dec. 4, 1919.

Dear Eddie:

Well Eddie, its a week since you heard from me last so I thought I would take my pen in hand to let you know something about the market.

Its the luckiest thing in the world for you that you aint here to see what rotten executions all your customers is getting. Always sold at the lowest and bought at the highest. Before you know it all the customers will go on strike. It seems to be all the rage this year like the influenza and the shimmy. Its being done, so to speak. Well, honest Eddie, the way some of the accounts are being handled while youre away is something terrible. As one feller says it: "It couldnt be worse even if Eddie was here himself." I dont know whether thats a compliment or a knock. Figure it out yourself.

Listen, Eddie, I have been reading some high class books lately because I got them free with a subscription to a magazine, and some of the stuff is pretty good, so I made up some maxims which you should have framed, and hung up in your customers room:

"All that glitters aint Union Pacific"

"He who hesitates, don't pay no commissions"

"A cash profit in the bank is worth double it on paper with your broker"

"Love your neighbour as yourself, but leave his tips alone"

What do you think of them? Maybe I should send them to some financial magazine, dont you think so? I know I got the talent.

What do you think of the market, or aint you seen the papers since you left New York for your vacation trip? Your assistant has been advising me to buy when theyre low and sell when theyre high. That's a good sensible young feller you got. He knows his business.

After this I'm going to follow his advice and buy at the bottom and sell at the top. They tell me if you keep on doing that you never lose money. Is that a positive fact?

Yours, etc.,
JOE.

P.S. How can you tell when stocks is at the bottom or at the top?
P.S. I thought there was some catch to it.
P.S. Here's another one "A check in time saves your margin!"

Clem's Comment:

Not a bad set of maxims from Joe. Is he actually learning? Investing and trading is a skill game and Joe is certainly practicing enough, so he should get better at it, even if it is to just stop.

"He who hesitates, don't pay no commissions"

He is catching on. Especially for the trader, there is always another opportunity around the corner.

Now if only I could beam back my *101 Ways to Pick Stock Market Winners* to him, he might learn how to catch the bottom of a stock.

If only he would read more books, he might stop losing so much money.

But no, it is just not going to happen, is it?

New York, Dec. 12, 1919.

Dear Eddie:

I hope this letter reaches you in Chicago where your office said you would stop for a few weeks to open up a branch office. What's the matter, are you trying to expand your business like the United Cigar stores. First thing you know, you'll be giving away coupons with every hundred shares of stock, redeemable in five years for a handsome tombstone, which probably comes in handy at that time.

I wish you would see Moe Sachs while you're in Chicago because last time I seen him he wasn't satisfied with the way Sanger, Gottlieb & Co. were handling his business. He's a big trader, Eddie, so your firm would thank you if you got him for a customer. If you see him tell him you know me and that your Sophie is a sister of my Flora's nephew. I think he is related in some way to me, though I aint held it against him none at all. No fooling though, Eddie, if you get his account, all his friends will come in after him. Treat them right because if they're satisfied they go to the limit! I know because before Ike Gottlieb retired they used to trade in everything in and out all the time. The firm made more in commissions than the customers made on profits! Gee, it must be a great game this brokerage business.

Whats new in Chicago? Has the people gotten over the Cincinnati revolution yet? Say Eddie, I was in Chicago the day before the World Series commenced, and those fellers were so cocky, you'd think Christy Mathewson and Ty Cobb never lived. Their chests was so full of wind, every time they exhaled I put up my coat collar. I'll tell you one thing, I made more money out of that World Series than I made in the stock market in my life!

Eddie, I havent done something in the market in such a long time I wouldn't know what to buy or sell so if you hear something let me know over the wire. I hear lots of pools is operating from Chicago. Studebaker, they tell me, will go to 250. I suppose they can do it too. After Keystone and Savoid, I'll believe anything once.

Drop me a line, or send me a flash over the wire. Flora sends her love. Fannie says to buy her something from Marshall Field, and Milton wants me to ask you if you will stop in the Blackstone to see what color the carpet is in the dining room. He says he has a bet on it.

Yours, etc.,

JOE.

P.S. What do you think about buying some Pere Marquette?

P.S. Would you buy that rather than Invincible Oil?

P.S. I want to make a lot of money on little capital, in a short time, without risk. So do 100,000,000 other people, hey Eddie?

Clem's Comment:

"I want to make a lot of money on little capital, in a short time, without risk. So do 100,000,000 other people, hey Eddie?"

Joe really is catching on. Making money in a short time, with little capital and no risk is simply not an option.

Meanwhile Joe has made a killing on the rigged 1919 World Series Baseball. It seems like rigged games are easier to win than trading on Wall Street.

That's probably true, but once again most gamblers don't understand they don't lose by being wrong, they lose because of the "over round."

The over round is the percentage take the bookie will make whoever wins, it's the difference between paying out 100% of stakes received and maybe 90%. The over round is created by making odds that don't equate to 100%. Imagine playing heads and tails. You bet $10 on heads. If you lose you lose $10, if you win you win $9.

I'll play book maker on that game all day long. What is more, someone will take my odds all day long too. Degenerate gamblers just want to play and while playing this example game looks stupid, trading stocks looks and feels kind of impressive and sophisticated. Such is the allure of playing the market.

Brooklyn, N. Y., Dec. 18, 1919.

Dear Eddie:

I can't seem to get you on the telephone these days because every time I call up, your secretary says your out, or maybe your tied up in a conference, or a Directors meeting, or out to lunch, or something else. That's a great game, Eddie, and it must work beautiful with strangers, and everything, also book agents, insurance men, advertising solicitors, and bill collectors, but don't think you can fool your poor relations with that cheap stuff.

I am writing you to find out what you think of the market because I am hung up with some stocks, and don't know whether I should dump them or hold on. Their names are Marine common and Sinclair, which I suppose you have heard about sometime or other. Well, about the Marines I got them since the boys made them famous over in France. I only hope I don't have to hold it until another war makes the name popular again. The other stock is making me crazy in the head. It's that question about "rights." Do you know anything about "rights?"

I've been reading the financial pages and special books on the market so as in order to find out about these here "rights" and finally I think I got what it means only I want to tell you so you can tell me whether I'm right or wrong. Here it is. A "right" is something which a feller has when he has a stock, and which if he don't want it, he can sell it to another feller who maybe is anxious for it. Sometimes they can be sold for a bunch of money and other times they aint worth the paper their printed on. Also if a feller don't want to do what he's got the "right" to do, he can use it just the same, and get some more stock which he don't want, because he's got enough already, so he sells what he gets extra.

Very simple.

Do you think its time to buy or sell stocks? I see by the papers that the money market is very tight. That don't surprise me none. I know lots of people which is in the same class, and one feller's named Eddie. Now don't get sore. I don't mean nothing at all. Anyway I see money is first 6% and then 10%, and like nothing it jumps to 20%, only to flop back to 5% near the end of the day. I wish I could find out what's it all about. It seems that every time money goes up, stocks go down. Ike Simon says all the Bank Presidents sold their stocks six months ago, and when the market kept on going up they got sore, and now they're trying to break the market with tight money so they can get their stocks back again. Is that right? It certainly don't look like the public was getting a square deal in Wall Street, but that's nothing new for Wall Street – or the public.

With regards from the family to your family,

Yours, etc.,
JOE.

P.S. Come out to see our new house. We got two bathrooms!
P.S. Aint interest charges ever coming down, Eddie?
P.S. I know about one "right" which you'll never get me to sell, and that is the "right" to call you and your firm everything under the sun whenever you deserve it, and which is every day.

Clem's Comment:

Rights issue are still to this day a confusing matter. Companies have rights issues because, generally speaking, they are out of cash and credit. They don't of course say that, they have all kinds of fine reasons why they need more money. However, they didn't need the money, nothing changed much or nothing important enough for them to mention, then they did.

If I sound like Joe there is a good reason.

However, rights can be very good for an investor if they buy in before the rights are announced because the ending of a nagging uncertainty about the company's finances will add value to the share. The company will offer the shares at a knock down price, so the investor will get a blast of upside and with luck a positive run for the stock over the following period.

This phenomenon is of course reserved for properly run large companies. At the more aromatic end of the market, which undoubtedly will attract the likes of Joe, these tendencies need not apply.

Meanwhile there is a credit squeeze going on which is hurting the market fuelled by credit. 90 years later it was just such a credit squeeze, or rather freeze, that crashed the markets and brought the developed world to the point of economic collapse.

Can nothing have really changed?

Atlantic City, Dec. 26, 1919.

I can't think of a name worse enough to call those thieves what put money up to 30 per cent so that in order to make everything go down, and clean me out completely. The dirty murderers, the loafers, honest, Eddie, words fail me. I think this letter should of been written on asbestos paper, because before I am through it will be so hot, it should burn up before you get it.

And my business! I can't think of it at all. Last week I drawn down all my profits to protect my account with your firm which was sending me margin calls every five minutes.

Its a fine good thing the market finally stopped going one way. I thought maybe it forgot to buy a return ticket. Believe me, it made no stops, and moved like a express train anxious to get somewhere in a hurry quick. Oh, Eddie, such a headache I had last night I couldn't sleep, and my Flora kept on asking me was anything wrong and I said "No." May I never tell such another lie in my life, that is should I live. And I aint sure of that.

You know that $1500 diamond and ruby breast pin I gave Flora for her last birthday? Well, tomorrow I must ask her to give it to me back, because I need the cash like a race horse needs four legs.

What shall I do now? I don't know whether its easier to jump off the roof of the Traymore or take carbolic acid right on the boardwalk. Only last week I had a nice profit and I wanted to take it, but your manager here said for me to take my time because big things was going to happen and there would be a quick move. I never knew that stocks move two ways, up and down, and when they started to go down, honest to God, Eddie, I was paralyzed. Anyway so I comes in this morning to collect the ruins, and your manager greets me with one of those sour pickle grins and says "Well Joe, that was a fine healthy re-action we had in the market, ain't it?" I could have killed him.

Eddie, I want to tell you something. I'm through! Understand, Eddie? I'm through. Not another share I buy or sell. Finished!

Absolutely done! Don't send me no more tips. Don't send me no more margin calls. Don't send me no more statements. Don't send me no more of anything. Which reminds me, did you lose anything personally on this break? I don't wish you no hard luck but I hope you got to hock your gold watch and chain, and that reminds me again of Flora's breast pin, and my heart starts knocking like a riveter. What shall I tell her? How must I explain it, and who can I blame, besides you?

Thats some wonderful advice you gave me last week. Every day the market broke you said it was the last, and they couldn't go any lower. I guess they wasn't listening to what you said, hey Eddie! What you don't know about stocks would fill the Congressional Library. I'm through.

JOE.

P.S. I suppose now that I'm cleaned out, the market will go up again. That's always the way. In at the top and out at the bottom, like a elevator which travels only one way.
P.S. I wouldn't mind being broke if it only don't happen at Atlantic City where I can't borrow a nickel and my partner won't let me draw in advance.
P.S. Listen, if you know of something SURE I could buy or sell quickly to make up some of my loss send me a wire right away.

Clem's Comment:

Every would-be trader should keep a copy of this piece in their pocket. This is gambler's ruin. This IS what it feels like to blow yourself up in the market. It might be for $1,000 or all your worth, the feeling is the same, but the scale can wipe you out permanently.

Untold speculators gambling with leverage have been destroyed this way. Every market correction scythes downs thousands from the richest to the poorest.

It doesn't have to happen.

Every time you want to go boots in to a trade, read this.

Atlantic City, Jan. 2, 1920.

Dear Eddie:

Well Eddie, thank God the market has stopped going down, for a few minutes anyway. If it had gone down any more you would find me selling newspapers on Broadway and Houston Street; that is if someone would be good enough to lend me enough money to buy some first. Your margin clerk called me for money so many times during the break in the market, it sounded like his echo. Never was he satisfied when I told him my credit was good, and even if it wasn't he shouldn't have gotten so mad about it.

Well, Eddie, what do you think of things now? Do you think the market has gone down enough, and it will come back soon, or will it go still lower? If you think the bottom is out of it and there will be another smash, let me know what to sell short, so I can give you a order. Of course you aint got no margin in my account now, but if you're going to sell something instead of buying it, it don't take no money, so you don't need no margin. In fact, while I think of it, if you sell something it brings you in some money don't it, so then you can credit some of it to my account.

Flora is all upset about her diamond breastpin, which I wrote you in my last letter I got to sell so in order to get enough money to pay our hotel bills here. I finally didn't tell her I was broke in the market but told her the mounting on the breastpin was out of date, and the setting was loose, and I didn't want her to lose it, so she better let me have it to take to a jeweller. Of course I didn't tell her that the jeweler I took it to gave me a ticket instead of a receipt. If she ever finds out, you can tell my Lodge to tell the members to send no flowers.

Some of the fellers here from St. Louis and Cleveland is afraid to go back to their homes. When they left for Atlantic City they was AA-No. 1 – at least $50,000 to $100,000 – 10 days dating, but now! Spot cash or a certified check wouldn't buy for them a $100 bill of goods. They all told me that was the last time they would buy stocks in Wall Street. That's what they all said three years ago, but I notice they got awful poor memories. I hope they don't forget to pay me back the money I loaned them to go home. I aint got much left, but I wouldn't have them disgrace themselves by wiring for money, besides which they will maybe remember the good turn I done them and buy some goods from my firm when they got money again. Anyway the wish is the father and mother of the thought. So long. There's nothing new. I hope its the same by you, and I remain, yours, etc.,

JOE.

P.S. Don't tell nobody about the diamond breastpin.

P.S. Why don't you buy that nice pearl stick pin I got. Its worth to-day $1,200 if its worth a cent.

P.S. Ask Ike Heim if he still wants to buy those lots I got in Floral Park. They're dirt cheap at half the price.

Clem's Comment:

In politics it's called a transfer payment. A transfer payment is when resources are taken from one group and transferred to another. This might be from industry to agriculture or from the rich to the poor. Here the transfer payment is from commerce to Wall Street.

Joe is clearly a grafter. He is a wheeler and dealer. It is natural for him to think he can wheel and deal the market. Sadly the market is not a negotiation, it's a non-negotiable transaction. This is where many wheeler dealers come unstuck.

The markets are asocial, which is why the left wing hates them. Markets are cold. You can't plead with them, you can't renegotiate with them, you can't bamboozle them, you can't intimidate them for long. You can buy or sell and you are either right or wrong. It's a skill game played against the best, where the umpire and scorer is your profit and loss statement.

You can't beat the market. You can however make good returns; for that you have to work with the market and a good place to start is by avoiding making your broker rich, which is exactly what Joe has done.

Chicago, Ill., Jan. 7, 1920.

Dear Eddie:

Well, here I am at last in the Windy City they call it, probably because you have just spent three weeks here. I've met some of your friends here, Eddie, and from what they tell me, you didn't spend anything else.

This is a funny city, if I do say so myself. Everything they got must got to be larger or better, or classier, or finer than New York. And when you are on Michigan Avenue five minutes with a native he makes you believe Fifth Avenue is worse than Main Street in Cornupolis, Ohio, and Broadway is a cheap imitation of something or other in Chicago. I forget what they got that compares with Broadway. I aint ever seen anything anywhere that compares with our Gay White Milky Way. All of which I suppose don't interest you none because it has nothing to do with the market, besides which your firm has opened a branch in Chicago, and you would be more interested if I would write you something about how the business is going on since you went back to New York, hey Eddie?

Well, Ill tell you. You got fine offices. The cuspidors shine all over so you can see your face in them. Everything looks like a regular bank. It must have cost your firm a small fortune. But you got a margin clerk there which is just as worse than the one you got in New York. He wanted 20 points on Steel, when all the other houses here only ask 15 points, and some 10. I brought some of my relatives with me to open accounts, but they aint no Rockefellers, understand, and 20 points on Steel they don't know at all!

What do they think of the market in New York? Every broker here thinks the New York brokers a bunch of burglars which would put Jimmy Valentine and Jesse James in the kindergarten class. Not an order to buy or to sell which don't hear no holler. They're so used to kicking on executions, they complain before even the market opens. The day I was in there one customer which bought 1,000 Rubber in the morning, sold it around noon, brought it back and sold it again at the close. After deducting commissions and taxes, he figured he made about $500. You should of seen how happy he was! But he didn't stop to figure that the firm made $600 in commission on his trades alone. If that was your new manager which advised this feller to trade in and out like that, he must make several million more than expenses. Pretty soft!

Yours, etc.,

JOE.

P.S. The people here walk lop-sided from carrying chips on their shoulders.
P.S. Would you advise the purchase of Southern Pacific?
P.S. Be generous with your information. I never act on it anyway.

Clem's Comment:

Joe has certainly made a quick comeback from being wiped out in the credit crunch crash of 1919-20. Gamblers will always find a way. However Joe has picked up the fact that costs equal losses, which is a large step towards salvation, because the market can be in your favour if you don't spend all its profits on the costs of trading. If you never grasp that you are doomed.

He also has inklings that more brokers have yachts than traders, or as they say in the UK: Why do bookmakers drive Rolls Royces?

It is important, however, to remember that Joe is not an investor. The period in which he is losing his shirt leveraging himself up with margin and trading away, was perfect for solid respectable investing.

Lakewood, N. J., Jan. 15, 1920.

Dear Eddie:

Well, Eddie, old boy, the market is pretty good these days, aint it? All the time its going lower and lower, and with me being short of the market, it don't give me no worry none at all whatever, only I hope by the time I get ready to take my profits the firm won't be busted. That would be a terrible thing, wouldn't it, Eddie?

Say, Eddie, what do you know all about Foreign Exchange business, and isn't it a good time to leave the here Marks and Franks alone? But if these Marks were worth nearly a quarter before the war and now you can buy them at two cents, shouldn't a feller take a flyer maybe on say $10 or $20 worth. Ike Levy advises me to wait until they are two for a cent like peanuts, and told me if you buy them then and they go down to nothing you can use them for book-marks. I don't see no joke in it, but Ike is still laughing his sides out at his funny remark.

I tell you what, Eddie, I think the Germans are forcing the Marks down and down so we will all buy them, and so that everybody in all the other countries will also buy them, because when the whole world is financially interested in Marks, they got to be considerate to the German people because otherwise they won't get their money back. As Booth Tarkingstein once said it "Where the money lies, goes the heart out!"

What do you think of the City of Paris take-a-chance bonds, which you can buy cheap and maybe win a prize of 100,000 Franks, if you got a pull with the Minister of Finance. Besides which they must be safe, because I am told Paris is doing a very good business just now and should be a fine first-class concern with a Bradstreet or maybe Dun high credit rating.

Would you buy or sell Sterling, and why? I can't understand any of this business. All I hear is that the pound is going lower and lower, but I can see that any day at our butcher, which must be studying this foreign exchange business right along the rotten weight we get on our soup meat.

With love from the family, and hoping you aint been taking any wooden alcohol, I am

Yours, etc.,

JOE.

P.S. If Marks go down to one cent buy me a quarters worth.

P.S. Give me a good stock to buy or sell, and if it turns out right I will take all the credit.

P.S. If it turns out wrong I will blame you.

Clem's Comment:

Oh noooo Joe is discovering Forex trading. He is finally getting the knack of stocks, after much investment in his harsh education and he looks like he might jump into Forex as clueless as he was in stock trading.

It is interesting to note that this letter refers to the beginning of the German hyperinflation, when Germany destroyed its economy in a kind of QE where the government ended up monetising any kind of corporate bond offered to it to stoke the economy and wreck reparations to the victorious allies.

Whether Joe has the answer to his trading strategy is an open question. Sometimes it can be a mental thing. He is for example sitting pat on his short positions and not churning his account, a good start. So who knows, Joe might be a master short trader. As long as he can keep away from Forex he might be OK.

Lakewood, N. J., Jan. 21, 1920.

Dear Eddie:

What hit the market yesterday? Was it maybe a sledge hammer or the Equitable Building? When I looked at my paper last night and seen all those minuses, I thought maybe the financial editor ran out of plus signs because he had a big demand for them last week. Well, anyway, Eddie, thank God, I aint worried none. All the stocks you advised me to buy I sold short, and if you got heart failure because you think I am thinking of committing suicide, don't get excited, because this is the first time I am really making some real money. Only I am still worried about your firm, and will they really give the money when I want to take my profit. Last time I had a big profit with another firm in Wall Street they stopped doing business just when I was going to cash in. They had such nice carpets and furniture too!

Say, Eddie, I just found out something. A feller just told me that lots of fellers was purposely taking losses so as in order to deduct them from their profits and make them smaller, so they won't have to pay such large income taxes. Now I know why you was taking all those losses for me all summer, only you took so much losses they was more than my profits, so now I figure the Government owes me money.

Buy me some Wheeling & Lake Erie at the market. I have inside information the Rockefellers have been buying it because they got oil on their properties, which they aint found it yet, but they are on the tracks!

Is there any change in the foreign exchange situation? Everybody is talking about, and everybody is worried about it, so I guess its all right for me to be talking and worried about it too, even if I don't care about it two cents.

What interest is your firm charging me this month. If you make it one penny more than 7 per cent. I'll transfer my account, and oblige

Yours, etc.,

JOE.

P.S. Can I charge my stock market losses against my firm's profits on ladies' sports coats?

P.S. Can I transfer my profits to my wife's account?

P.S. I just got your statement which I see you charge me only 10 per cent. Kirschbaum & Kahn charged 11 per cent.

Clem's Comment:

Perhaps a happy ending. However, you can see Joe wandering away from his successful formula, which is a classic mistake. If you get an investing or trading formula, keep at it until it stops working. Never stop trading a successful formula because you get bored.

Trading, or speculating as it was known, is a hard game; perhaps ten times harder to make money at than investing. I like to say it pays out double what you can get from investing if you master the art.

So the thing to do is invest. Then when you can make 15-20% a year investing, you'll be good enough to take a shot at trading. Before you can make that level of profit investing, you've little chance of succeeding at trading.

P.S. good luck and don't follow Joe or for that matter Eddie, or the Sumatra boys.

ABOUT THE AUTHORS

The publishers were unable to contact Mr Kustomer as they went to press.

Clem Chambers is CEO of ADVFN, Europe and South America's leading financial website.

A broadcast and print media regular, Clem Chambers is a familiar face and frequent co-presenter on CNBC and CNBC Europe. He is a seasoned guest and market commentator on BBC News, Fox News, CNBC Arabia Newsnight, Al Jazeera, CNN, SKY News, TF1, Canada's Business News Network and numerous US radio stations.

He is renowned for calling the markets and predicted the end of the bull market back in January 2007 and the following crash. He has appeared on ITV's News at Ten and Evening News discussing failures in the banking system and featured prominently in the Money Programme's Credit Crash Britain: HBOS — Breaking the Bank and on the BBC's City Uncovered: When Markets Go Mad.

Clem has written investment columns for Wired Magazine, which described him as a 'Market Maven', The Daily Mail, The Daily Telegraph and The Daily Express and currently writes for The Scotsman, Forbes, RiskAFRICA, Traders and YTE.

He was The Alchemist – stock tipster – in The Business for over three years and has been published in titles including: CityAM, Investors Chronicle, Traders Magazine, Stocks and Commodities, the Channel 4 website, SFO and Accountancy Age and has been quoted in many more publications including all of the main UK national newspapers. He also wrote a monthly spread betting column in gambling magazine Inside Edge for over a year.

Clem has written several books for ADVFN Books, including 101 Ways To Pick Stock Market Winners and A Beginner's Guide to Value Investing.

In the last few years he has become a financial thriller writer, authoring The Twain Maxim, The Armageddon Trade, Kusanagi and The First Horseman.

Clem also writes for the ADVFN newspaper and has a premium newsletter for subscribers, the **Diary of a Contrarian Investor** (http://www.advfn.com/newsletter/clemchambers/).

ALSO BY CLEM CHAMBERS

The Death of Wealth:
The Economic Fall of the West

by Clem Chambers

Was 2012 the beginning of the end for western wealth? Best-selling author and Forbes columnist Clem Chambers puts the markets in review and explains the forthcoming crises. Anthologising his writings from the past year, *The Death of Wealth* is the essential guide to the emerging financial landscape.

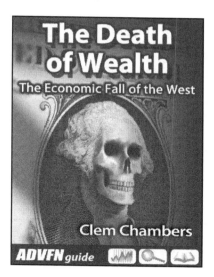

ADVFN Guide:
The Beginner's Guide to Value Investing

by Clem Chambers

The stock market is not only for rich people, or those intent on gambling. 'Value Investing' is how Warren Buffet became the richest man in the world. A method of investing in the stock market without taking crazy risks, 'Value Investing' will help you build your fortune, no matter the economic climate. Perfect for novice investors, the book clearly outlines how to choose the best stocks and how – thanks to the Internet. It is the perfect way to ensure you 'get rich slow' with minimal stress.

ADVFN Guide:
101 Ways to Pick Stock Market Winners

by Clem Chambers

101 tips to help day traders, investors and stock pickers to focus on what characterises a potentially successful stock. Personally researched by Clem Chambers, one of the world's leading authorities on market performance. Incisive, brutally honest and occasionally very funny, *101 Ways to Pick Stock Market Winners* is an invaluable manual for anyone wanting to make money out of the markets.

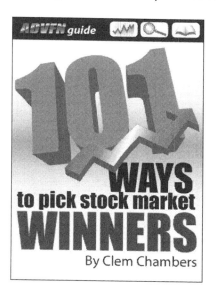

Go to www.advfnbooks.com for more information on these titles.

OTHER TITLES FROM ADVFN BOOKS

Lessons From The Financial Markets For 2013

by Zak Mir

Learn from all the suspense, mania and gloom of one of the markets' most dramatic years. In *Lessons From The Financial Markets For 2013* Zak Mir puts all his charting expertise to practice and analyses the key stocks, markets and events to provide an essential preview of 2013. By exploring the highlights and the lowlights of 2012 you can learn vital lessons to help make the best investment choices, now and in the future.

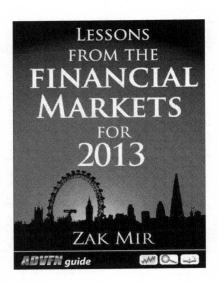

101 Charts for Trading Success

by Zak Mir

Using insider knowledge to reveal the tricks of the trade, Zak Mir's *101 Charts for Trading Success* explains the most complex set ups in the market. Illustrated with easy to understand charts this is the accessible, essential guide of how to read, understand and use charts to buy and sell stocks; a must for all future investment millionaires!

Lessons From The Trader Wizard

by Bill Cara

New from trading legend and the Free Market Patriot Bill Cara, *Lessons From The Trader Wizard* teaches the tactics and skills to beat Wall Street. Bill shows you how to navigate the new world of trading the capital markets.

Evil's Good:
Book of Boasts and Other Investments

by Simon Cawkwell

Britain's most feared bear-raider spots overvalued stocks, shorts them and goes for the kill. He's been known to make £500,000 in a single week. In *Evil's Good* – part auto-biography, part financial training guide – Simon Cawkwell tells all of his market triumphs (and downfalls) and describes the 'shorting' rules that have made him so wealthy.

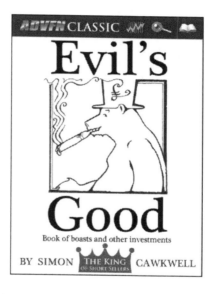

Go to www.advfnbooks.com for more information on these titles.

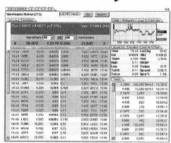

Made in the USA
Middletown, DE
25 September 2016